T0078375

WHERE
IS MY *Bride?*

EVANGELINE RENTZ

WESTBOW
PRESS®
A DIVISION OF THOMAS NELSON
& ZONDERVAN

WestBow Press books may be ordered through booksellers or by contacting:

WestBow Press
A Division of Thomas Nelson & Zondervan
1663 Liberty Drive
Bloomington, IN 47403
www.westbowpress.com
844-714-3454

ISBN: 978-1-6642-1730-0 (sc)
ISBN: 978-1-6642-1732-4 (hc)
ISBN: 978-1-6642-1731-7 (e)

Library of Congress Control Number: 2020925402

Print information available on the last page.

WestBow Press rev. date: 01/05/2021

In Loving Memory of my Mother
Evangelist Annie Mae Rentz
March 25, 1941 – January 11, 2020

Mama and Me

Mama, you were truly one of my greatest gifts from God outside of salvation. Your love, prayers, support, guidance, wisdom, encouragement, correction, discipline and the very life you lived have helped to mold me into the woman that I am today. Your faith, strength and determination to embrace the word of God and to unapologetically serve your Lord and Savior Jesus Christ with fervent tenacity laid an incredible example and blueprint that I proudly follow and emulate. You have been my greatest inspiration and I miss your physical presence tremendously.

We (your children) talk regularly, and we often laugh at how your words, wisdom and example continues to speak, guide, and correct us on a daily basis, even from your heavenly resting place. Thank you for the journey we shared together. God could not have chosen a more perfect mother and grandmother for the children and grandchildren born of this Rentz clan. We love and miss you. Continue to rest in Jesus.

Contents

Prayer for Angie's Book

In Loving Memory of My Precious Mother

Dear Father God:

I come to You in the holy and powerful name of my Lord and Savior Jesus Christ, and by the authority of the name of Jesus. Father God, I lay my daughter Evangeline and Your book that You inspired her to write, down at Your altar.

I am asking You Father, that You pour Your holy anointing oil and Your anointing glory over Angie, and over each and every page of Your book, so that readers will see Your light and feel Your Glory ... and that Your Words draw them close to You.

Father allow this book to touch the hearts and souls of many throughout this world, for this generation and generations for years to come. Allow the readers to be blessed Father God, in the presence of Your Glory. Let them feel You my Lord ... let them feel You near. I pray for the readers Father, that they not only hear Your words in this book, but Father I pray that they be doers of Your word also.

Now Lord God Almighty, I pray for Angie, that You keep her and strengthen her. Lord I know that it is not always easy doing the assignments that You have chosen us to do, but Father, I remember you saying, " ...I will never leave you nor forsake you," (Hebrew 13:5 NKJV), so I pray for Angie. Keep her Father ... keep her Lord God; keep her with Your word and from the evil of the world. Lord, let Angie always lean on You.

Now Almighty God, I pray for all those, who have helped and encouraged Evangeline in this assignment. Bless them Father God; for they have embraced Your child.

Now Jehovah Jireh, our Provider; Jehovah Rapha, our Healer; You heal our diseases. Jehovah Nissi, our battle fighter, our victory. You are our Banner. Jehovah Shalom, our peace. Jehovah Rohi, our Shepherd, You are the good Shepherd, You gave Your life for Your sheep. Jehovah Tsidkenu, our righteousness.

Now Lord: El Shaddai; our Eternal God; El Elyon; the most high God, possessor of heaven and earth; El ohim; our merciful God, I lay all of this in Your eternal hands, believing in Your word and trusting in Your mercy.

In the holy name of Jesus, I pray, Your child
and servant Annie Mae. Amen
(Excerpt from the book **Intimate Moments**)

Written by Evangelist Annie Mae Rentz
March 25, 1941 – January 11, 2020

Foreword

By: Linda Blackshear Smith

I have known Evangelist Evangeline "Angie" Rentz for over 20 years. I know that God orchestrated our meeting. Angie was a student in a Vacation Bible Class in which I was the Instructor. When she told me her name, I immediately knew that she was destined for working and serving greatly in God's Kingdom. And it fills me with much joy to witness Angie fulfilling my expectations. And it is a blessing and an honor to witness my friend consistently and steadfastly abiding by the Biblical principles that she so emphatically proclaims.

In her first book, *Intimate Moments*, Angie provided readers a how-to-manual for forming and sustaining Christian-based relationships. This follow-on book – *Where Is My Bride?* – extends her "manual." To be specific, using Paul's description of the relationship between the Christian church (the Bride) and Jesus (the Bridegroom), Angie develops a comprehensive set of operating principles for Christian-based marriages. Her compelling narrative invites readers to be reflective: *Do I have a clear understanding of God's design for Marriage? Is marriage a covenant with God?* Angie in her absolute resolve of not *sugarcoating* the truth makes it clear that God did not design marriage to be easy. "Marriage, like the thorny rose bush, can be both *exquisite and excruciating.*" It must be handled with care. Or, as Paul might ask, *Am I a Bride worthy of the Bridegroom?*

Many of us, Angie argues, do not give sufficient thought to preparing ourselves to be a good bride or a good groom, finding ourselves in relationships and marriages untethered to God's will. We have not spent those *intimate moments* with God seeking His counsel and asking, *Is this the one that God has prepared for me? What do I need to change?* Fortunately, Angie has written a principled guide and practical instructions to preparing readers for "Godly" marriages and for the return of Jesus Christ (the Bridegroom).

This book is a must read, for the single person—contemplating marriage, for the married persons—seeking to bring their marriage into God's favor, and for the Beloved Saint who is aware that we must prepare for the return of the Bridegroom.

There is no doubt that Angie's desire for us to be ready for our *Bridegroom* is genuine and heartfelt. It is indeed a great honor for me to recommend Angie' book, *Where Is My Bride?* This Book has stirred in me a passion to have a *Godly* marriage and to intentionally make proper preparations for the return of our Bridegroom-Christ Jesus.

Linda "Jewel" Blackshear Smith, NHA
Founder and President, Divinely Empowered Equipped Ministries
Author, *My Testimony*

Introduction

Marriage, who needs it? Seriously, what is it about a marital relationship that benefits society? Why are men and women still desperately longing to be a part of this covenantal relationship? Well, truthfully most little girls still fantasize about that big wedding day. The day she "slays" in that one special wedding gown. The day she walks down the aisle to connect with the man of her dreams. The day she chose to live "happily ever after" with the man that stole her heart.

It is an incredible dream. Unfortunately, very few actually experience the happily ever after. The memory of that beautiful day often ends in a bitter divorce or for many, has yet to even take place at all. Does this mean that successful marriages are no longer a vital part of our society? Should we just accept the world's viewpoint that successful covenantal relationships are now extinct? I think not. As a matter of fact, I know not.

Marriage is a covenant that was designed by God. Therefore, marriages are still essential, necessary and a beautiful part of the Kingdom of God. Earthly marriages were designed to be a physical representation of Christ's relationship with the church body. It represents oneness, trust and intimacy. It is an intimate relationship between two individuals that requires intentional actions in order to establish an unbreakable bond. However, we sadly make the mistake of attempting to establish this physical bond before establishing the spiritual bond with our "First Love." (Revelation 2:4 KJV)

As a single Christian woman, I was reminded that my strong desire to become a wife and mother is not wrong; it just should not be my most important priority. The reality is, I was born for a specific purpose, and that is to worship, serve and praise God. That is my number one goal and purpose. Consequently, fulfilling my purpose for the Kingdom of God should always be my primary focus. With that said, establishing an intimate relationship with my Savior and Lord must come first over my desire for establishing an earthly relationship. As a result, I intentionally began to focus on building my relationship with Jesus and as a result, the love and attention that He pours in my life was and still is amazing.

Since that moment, I am constantly sitting and spending intimate moments with God. I read, study, pray and literally have conversations with my Lord and Savior. We actually talk about everything and truthfully, we are not always pleased with each other's thoughts or actions; however, I do believe we always respect and cherish our time together. Let me be clear, the Lord is always patient, clear and honest with me. I choose to accept Him as the Lord of my life; therefore, I had to make a decision to listen, accept and follow His lead, even when I do not understand or like His plan.

He frequently pours into my life, especially during moments when I am preparing to preach and teach His Word. I have grown to cherish these moments for I now know and understand how valuable and precious they truly are. You see, it is during these moments when my relationship with my Savior is strengthened. It is during these moments that my character continues to develop into the woman I was born to be and it is during these moments that I am truly challenged to walk in the example of Christ with the strength of the Holy Spirit in order to fulfill my purpose.

Several years ago, during one of my intimate moment encounters with the Lord, I sat focusing and meditating on Him as I desperately sought Him for clarity and revelation about a current assignment. I questioned His message and direction, yet I could not shake it. You see, this particular Word that filled my spirit was not going to be easy to swallow or receive for many people, including me. I remember praying, seeking, and waiting for confirmation. Yet, the assignment nor the message changed. Therefore, I knew I had to deliver it. Thus, I trusted the Lord to help me and to use me to present His Word with simplicity and in love.

So, please travel back with me to that moment in time. The moment when I heard the Lord speak clearly and precisely to me. An intimate moment in time when I heard the Lord whisper these words to my spirit.

My Dearest Pumpkin:

I am here, fear not, I will never leave you or forsake you. I understand your reservations about your current assignment, but My dear you must go. Stand firm and speak only the words that I tell you. Although uncomfortable, never forget that I am with you.

When you stand before the people ask them how long will they walk contrary to My word? My love for them is so great, yet they act as though I do not exist. Yes, I hear their prayers, and I read all the accolades of praises they post on their Facebook and social media pages. However, when I observe their actions and behaviors, I am of no existence.

Ask them what will it take for Me to become first in their lives? I protected them from dangers seen and unseen. I kept them in the midst of trials, tribulations, and turmoil. I healed their bodies; I raised their children; I provided a roof over their heads and food for their tables. It was I who paid the bill when they did not know where the money would come from and it was I who was there to comfort them in their lowest hour. No one will ever love them the way I do. Not only do I constantly whisper My love for them in their ears, I showed them My love when I suffered and died on Calvary.

When will they die for Me? My heart aches and I am crucified over and over every time I watch some of My leaders abuse their power by preaching for financial gain and failing to preach the uncompromised word of God. The pain of isolation and betrayal I felt as I journeyed up Golgotha torment Me every time a servant fails to visit the sick, feed the hungry, encourage the downtrodden or clothe the needy. I re-live that moment of suffering from the nails in My flesh every time I witness one of My leaders or ministers of the gospel, molest the children they oversee, fornicate, or have adulterous affairs with the people of the church. I feel the agony of the cross every single time I observe one of My Father's beautiful creations who has professed acceptance of Me gamble, lie, cheat, fornicate, do drugs, get an abortion, display mean hateful spirits towards others, and drink and party with the world instead of preaching, teaching, and drawing the world to repentance.

The pain is so great, and My love is so deep and sincere, yet what else can I do? I have laid the foundation and provided the opportunity that whoso ever will, can come to Me, because I love them. Pumpkin, I am watching and waiting for My bride. Make no mistake; I will know her when I see her, because she has prepared herself for that moment. Her love for Me is just as strong as My love for her; and her every moment is in preparation of Our union. My excitement constantly intensifies as I wait for that moment to arrive. What a glorious time it will be to finally become one with her.

So, my Pumpkin, you asked Me what should you tell the people? Just ask them for Me, Where is My Bride?

All My love,
The Bridegroom

Beloved, this message pierced my spirit in such a powerful way. My heart filled with sorrow as I remembered the many times, I hurt Him by disobeying His voice. I thought about His love and how He has blessed my life in so many ways and for so many years. I could not help but focus on how He has consistently delivered me from so many painful and sinful situations. How He has truly covered and protected me from dangers seen and unseen and how He truly has never left or forsaken me.

Yet, what amazed me most about this message that He poured in my heart that night was that He is excitedly awaiting that great and glorious day when He can return to receive His bride. My heart truly leaped with joy and was filled with excitement because I too have been preparing and patiently waiting for my special wedding day. But this message pierced my spirit and redirected my focus from exclusively dreaming and desiring an earthly marriage, to realizing that I have already been chosen to be a part of a glorious and magnificent spiritual marriage. Yes, this message confirmed within my spirit and helped me to recognize that one day I will indeed be a bride. Whether earthly or spiritual, there are no words to describe the overwhelming anticipation of that moment. So, I wait with purpose, with integrity and with love, as I prepare for my great wedding day!

1

In the Beginning

And behold, I am coming quickly, and My reward is with Me,
to give to everyone according to his work. I am the Alpha and
the Omega, the Beginning and the End, the First and the Last.
—Revelation 22:12–13 (NKJV)

A wedding ceremony is one of the most celebrated events in a person's life. And although I have never been married, I have spoken with many brides who proclaim with uniformed agreement that the wedding planning is extensive, detailed, and extremely exhausting. Those brides also indicate that the cost is oftentimes exorbitant, yet it has not stopped people from having weddings.

The wedding ceremony is a glorious affair. The sanctuary is always beautifully decorated. The bridesmaids and groomsmen are flawless, and the guests are plentiful, excited, and full of joy as they sit and await the uniting of the bride and groom. Now just for a moment I would like for you to envision the last wedding you attended. Think about that moment when you sat and awaited the entrance of the groom. But instead of the earthly groom walking in, the Bridegroom enters and walks to the front of His holy sanctuary.

He stands tall and proud with anticipation of the entrance of His bride. The music starts and the doors open; however, there is no bride! Why? Where can she be? The church is thriving and has an active membership, so where is the bride? Where is the one who "has made herself ready" (Revelation 19:7 NKJV)?

As I sit and reflect on the things that are currently going on in the world and in the church, I am not surprised by this simple yet complex question that the Lord whispered to my spirit. We have come to a place in time where we do what we want, live how we want, and still profess to be born-again believers. We live as though there are no guidelines, no boundaries, no rules, no repercussions, and no consequences for our lifestyles and choices. We have adopted and embraced the thought processes and characteristics of this sinful world. Therefore, there is no longer a desire nor a requirement to change.

We, the members of the local church, support leaders who openly vocalize statements of hatred, division, and discrimination. We have married deacons sending single female members emails asking them out on dates after searching for their information through the church registry. We have some pastors assigning their single female ministers and parishioners to married visiting preachers for comfort and enjoyment. We, the church, have professed saints showing up in church with someone's man or woman only to break out fighting in the sanctuary while the pastor is delivering the message. We have pastors and ministers traveling to conferences to meet up with women in their hotel rooms, deacons cursing out the pastor during leadership meetings, members smoking in the church parking lot, and seasoned saints guarding the kitchen while fussing over food and to-go plates.

Now although these are all true accounts of events that have taken place in the church, some of you are probably getting really upset with me right now. But it is OK. This book is not to judge but simply to help us reflect on these questions, our lifestyles, and our behaviors. Where is God's bride? Where is the *one* who has made herself ready?

I have witnessed church leaders rent buses and plan church trips to casinos in order to raise money for church anniversaries. We have pastors bullying members by using God's sacred pulpit to scold, lash out, degrade, and disrespect church members. And sadly, we have church members who house unforgiveness and choose to sow discord among the church body because of previous hurt and pain. And if this is not enough, there was a pastor who exclaimed that a certain musician was not welcomed in *his* church because he believed this person was actively participating in a homosexual relationship. Yet at the same time, he knowingly had church leaders in long-term sexual relationships outside the boundaries of marriage. Beloved, we, as born-again believers, cannot pick and choose which sins are acceptable and which sins are not. We must be willing to accept and embrace the fact that sin is sin, and the Lord hates all sin. So out of sincere love for you and obedience to God, I ask you once more, Where is God's bride? Where is the one who has made herself ready? Where is the one who embraces the entire Word of God? Where is the one who is actively preparing for His return?

In the book of Genesis, the world was introduced to human beings and animals. We were introduced to the moon, the sun, the land, and the sea. We were introduced to sex, family, sin, jealousy, and murder. It was in this book that lying, cheating, stealing, betrayal, envy, fornication, homosexuality, and adultery were all introduced. This book revealed the messy lives that humankind chose to live. It all started in the book of Genesis. Between the book of Genesis and the book of Revelation, there are sixty-four documented books that God provided as instruction and directives. Within these books God sent prophets, pastors, ministers, evangelists, teachers, and most importantly, God sent His son, Jesus, and the Holy Spirit to teach, guide, and lead His people to repentance and salvation. There was no situation or circumstance that was not addressed, explained, or dealt with.

Jesus came, He served, He taught, He healed, He visited, He embraced, He loved, He died, and He rose with all power in His hands for you, me, and all humankind. Within these books Jesus led by example and displayed the characteristics of a humble servant. However, when we get to the book of Revelation, we see Jesus in His glory as High Priest. The one who is in total control of His church.

> I was in the Spirit on the Lord's Day, and I heard
> behind me a loud voice, as of a trumpet, saying, I am

3

> the Alpha and the Omega, the First and the Last, and, What you see, write in a book and send it to the seven churches which are in Asia: to Ephesus, to Smyrna, to Pergamos, to Thyatira, to Sardis, to Philadelphia, and to Laodicea. Then I turned to see the voice that spoke with me. And having turned I saw seven golden lampstands, and in the midst of the seven lampstands One like the Son of Man, clothed with a garment down to the feet and girded about the chest with a golden band. (Revelation 1:10–13 NKJV)

The book of Revelation is the uncovering, the unveiling. In other words, it is the revelation of Jesus Christ. In chapter 1, Jesus speaks to His servant John and instructs him to send letters to the seven churches. In the midst of the seven churches (represented by the seven golden lampstands) stood one like the Son of Man, clothed in a garment down to His feet and girded about the chest with a golden girdle. It appears to be obvious to all of us that *Jesus is the light*; however, what does not seem to be to clear is that Jesus also expects us to be the light until He returns. "For you were once darkness, but now you are light in the Lord. Walk as children of light" (Ephesians 5:8 NKJV).

Jesus left us with responsibility. We are expected to be the light! Yet some of us are walking around so dim and dull until it is shameful. Well, in the book of Revelation Jesus is back, and He is standing in the midst of the churches, judging believers and looking for the light. We need to understand that in the book of Revelation, the Christ who interceded for us is gone. The Christ who intervened for us is gone. When Jesus returns, He returns for inspection and He will be walking in the midst of the churches searching for His bride—the one who has made herself ready. Now what does that really mean? What does it mean to make ourselves ready? This simply means to prepare for Christ's return. *Prepare* means to make ready for use. We must make ourselves ready for Christ to use us. Therefore, the question is, how do we do this? Well, let us go to the scriptures. In the scriptures, we learn that "if any man be *in Christ*, he is a new creature [creation]:

old things are passed away; behold, all things are become new" (II Corinthians 5:17 KJV; emphasis added).

Beloved, this particular preparation requires transformation. It requires becoming new creatures, which indicates that we become different people. We are not the same; we are now in Christ, and being in Christ means that Christ is now a part of us, our ways, and our actions. When we become new creatures [creations], we take on the characteristics of Christ. Think about this for a moment. Can we as Christians really be "in Christ" and not have similarities to Christ?

My biological mother is Annie Mae Rentz, and my biological father is Harry H. Rentz Jr. Therefore, my father's DNA and my mother's DNA are a part of who I am. My facial features, singing voice, and nurturing tendencies are compared to my precious mother. I am also told by many friends and family members that I have inherited my mother's excellent cooking and baking skills. Yet my pink lips, that unique gap in my teeth, and being left-handed are surely special gifts from my father. Consequently, if I did not have some resemblance or traits of those two individuals, people would question whether I am actually their birth child.

Therefore, it amazes me how we as professed Christians, born-again believers, can confess to be in Christ and look absolutely nothing like Him. We walk around constantly and consistently cursing, fussing, and lying. We choose to intentionally participate in infidelity and adulterous activities, knowingly choose to cheat on our income tax documentation, steal, and take things that do not belong to us, and many other activities that are too numerous to recount. Come on now, our actions should resemble those of Christ, right? Therefore, how can we be "in Christ" and walk around the house not speaking to our husband or wife for days. How can we choose to walk around defeated, depressed, excessively drinking, and constantly struggling with the same sins that we have been struggling with for the past five, ten, fifteen, or twenty years? How can we be a new creature when nothing about us has changed?

Now, please do not misunderstand me. I do not believe we are perfect beings who will never sin. In fact, the scriptures clearly state, "for all have sinned and fall short of the glory of God." (Romans 3:23

NKJV). However, I do believe the Bible teaches that our walk with Christ should result in deliverance, growth, and change. I do believe that as born-again believers the word of God teaches that our lifestyle and choices should be made to glorify God. Therefore, I do believe as new creations, we are to strive daily to make intentional decisions to fight against our fleshly cravings and desires that conflict with the Word of God. We should choose to trust and lean on the Lord as our strength and that we can trust Him because when we are "in Christ" He is our Keeper. "Now unto Him that is able to keep you from falling, and to present you faultless before the presence of His glory with exceeding joy" (Jude 24 KJV)

She made herself ready, which simply means, she went into preparation mode. Think about it, we do not just wake up, get dressed, and walk into our wedding ceremony; we must plan our wedding. We spend months, and months, and months, saving, planning, preparing, researching, and organizing. So why should we believe that there is no preparation expected for our spiritual marriage. Why would we believe that there is no expectation of planning or change for one of the most SIGNIFICANT EVENTS that will ever take place in our lives. Yes, salvation is free, but there was a price that was paid for our lives. And because of the price that was paid for our lives, we have a responsibility on how we choose to live our lives.

> *For you were bought at a price;*
> *therefore glorify God in your body*
> *and in your spirit, which are God's.*
>
> (I CORINTHIANS 6:20 NKJV)

When we think about an "earthly" bride preparing for her wedding, we see and many of us have experienced how much work this woman does to prepare for that one special day. She has to set the wedding date, get the marriage license, book the venue, set a budget, draft a guest list, hire a caterer, hire a photographer, hire a videographer, hire a florist, hire a band/musician, secure a wedding party, choose the attire for the wedding party, send out invitations, hire a wedding planner, choose a menu, order a cake, and hire a wedding decorator just to name a few. Now, prayerfully she is marrying a man who is fully engaged in assisting throughout this process. However, the point I am trying to make is that this woman cannot just get up, put on that beautiful wedding gown, show up to the church (venue) and walk down the aisle and expect to have a memorable wedding day. There are so many things that must be done before that big day.

Therefore, I do not understand how we, as the church body (the Bride of Christ), can get up, get dressed and come to church and sit down on the pew week after week, year after year and think it is alright with God. Some of us do absolutely nothing in preparation for His return.

Eve was created specifically to be a "help-meet" (helper) for Adam. Ruth was spotted and chosen by Boaz as she was busy working and gleaning the field. Rebecca was chosen as the wife for Isaac as she went down to the spring to draw water that she also served to Abraham's servant and his camels. And lastly, Esther found favor in all who saw her by the way she chose to use wisdom and take advice from Hegai, the King's Eunuch who was in charge. Esther was ultimately chosen as Queen and ended up saving her people because of her courage. These women did not just sit around doing nothing while waiting to become brides. They all operated in their purpose for God's Kingdom.

So why do we as the Bride of Christ believe that there is no work or preparation necessary. She Made Herself Ready. She was now "in Christ"; thus, she began to act like Christ and look like Christ because she was a part of Christ. We cannot do this thing called life our way. If we are born again believers, we willingly gave our life to Christ. This means we no longer have a life. We gave it away in exchange for an everlasting life with Christ. As a result, we must remember that the Lord has already established, designed, and laid out the way and plan for you and me. His way is righteousness. Christ represents holiness and righteousness; therefore, as His bride we also must chose to represent holiness and righteousness by following His plan and His design.

"Let us be glad and rejoice and give Him glory, for the marriage of the Lamb has come, and His wife has made herself ready." And to her it was granted to be arrayed in fine linen, clean and bright, for the fine linen is the righteous acts of the saints." (Revelation 19:7-8 NKJV). In this particular scripture, we see that as a result of her preparation the Lord allowed (granted) her the opportunity to wear fine linen. You see, she now looks like Him because of her life of holiness and righteousness. Therefore, He is now allowing her to be clothed like Him since she has become one with Him. Let's look at this for a moment: you see **first** He chose her, **then** she accepted to be His bride by choosing to follow His lead and by living according to His design and His way; **therefore**, as a result, He granted her permission to put on her wedding gown.

In the physical realm, when you think about a wedding ceremony there are many people in attendance; however, the bride is unmistakably recognizable. Without question, you know her when you see her. She stands above the crowd because of how she is dressed. Well, the same concept holds true in the spiritual realm. The bride of Christ should be easily identifiable because of how she is dressed. Wherever we go, in the streets, at the grocery store, on the job, or during a church service; no one should have to tell us who is the Bride of Christ. She will stand out above the crowd. We will know her and recognize her by the way she is dressed. This woman is clothed in righteousness, "….for He has clothed me with the garments of salvation, He has covered me with the robe of righteousness ……" (Isaiah 61:10 NKJV)

Listen Beloved, because I am chosen and because I have chosen to accept to live by the Lord's design of holiness and righteousness, I am now clothed in the garment of salvation. Which means I am now dressed, covered, and protected. I am dressed and in my wedding attire, prepared and waiting for the ceremony to begin. So, while I wait, I must constantly remind myself to be mindful and careful about my clothing. The scripture we read specifically indicates clean and bright. Think about it, whether you have already had the experience of wearing a wedding gown, or like me, patiently waiting on God's timing to wear that beautiful earthly garment, we all must agree that once that beautiful dress is firmly fitting upon our bodies, that we pay careful attention to our moves, actions, and surroundings in order to assure that the dress remains clean and spotless.

Well, the same care and attention must go to our spiritual wedding gown/garment. I have the responsibility to follow the Lord's example and <u>remain clean</u>. Yes, that is my responsibility. Can I do it without the help of the Lord? Absolutely not, but it is my responsibility to seek His voice, His direction, and His guidance and to follow and obey. This is the only way my garment will remain clean.

Now my brothers, I know when we mention brides we automatically think about women. However, in the spiritual realm the bride is the body of Christ and that covers male and female. We all have the same responsibility. Think about it, we must take time to pull the scriptures off the pages of the Bible and relate them to our everyday life. When we get dressed for an elaborate event, whatever the occasion, we are careful to make sure our clothing remains clean. We are intentional about everything we touch to make sure that no spots, blemishes, or residue is left behind on our clothing. It is our primary focus and desire to remain clean prior to and throughout the event.

For this particular scripture, I love the King James Version because it states, "clean and white." *"And to her was granted that she should be arrayed in fine linen, <u>clean and white</u>: for the fine linen is the righteousness of saints (Revelation 19:8 KJV)."* White represents purity, innocence, and birth in the scriptures. Remember, we are considered born-again believers, new creatures, old things have passed away. Therefore, the bride's clothing is clean and white for a reason. She is now one with Christ and she represents what He represents. In other words, she looks like Him. He represents Holiness and Righteousness, and so does His bride. Thus, as His bride, I must make a decision to look like He looks and to live like He lives. I cannot roll around in the dirt and think my outfit is going to stay clean. I cannot lie in the mud and think this beautiful garment is going to remain white. The Bridegroom is looking for the white. He is not looking for off-white, cream, seashell, or pecan tan. The Bible says clean and white which is the righteousness of the saints.

Make no mistake, we are not perfect and will definitely be tempted. We will more than likely be approached by some incredibly handsome and good-looking individuals who will present opportunities that will make our entire body yearn from the inside out. Trust me, I know, I have been there. Even though we know this person is not designed for our destiny, everything in us still screams and yearns to fall in their arms without thinking about any repercussions. Yet, we must have a made-up mind that we are determined that no matter what, our garment is going to stay clean. Therefore, we must make a decision that our love for Jesus will come before our wants to fulfill our fleshly desires.

The Bible teaches that Jesus came to earth and chose to die for our sins. He rose with all power in His hands. He is now sitting on the right side of God interceding on our behalf, and at the appointed time, He will return for His bride. He chose her and He set her aside for His glory and for His use. He now covers her, protects her, provides for her, and comforts her even before the ceremony. Why??? Because the engagement commitment is just as serious as the marriage (we will discuss this in a later chapter). Nevertheless, what we must remember now is because of our commitment, we must be determined in the physical realm and in the spiritual realm, that we are going to be prepared and ready for our husband.

Listen, if we are really going to be truthful; we realize that even in the physical realm, an earthly man does not want a dirty bride. Even when he may be the one in the dirt with her. He will oftentimes get up, dust himself off and go and find another woman to marry. So why would we think that Jesus wants a dirty bride. I do understand that Jesus tells us to come to Him as we are; however, when He steps into our life, He does not leave us the way we came. He cleans us up and begins to transform us from the inside out.

Now my brothers, as I said earlier, please do not miss the message by thinking this is only for women. Christ is coming back for His bride, the church, the body of believers. That is neither male nor female. It is the spiritual body of Christ. He is looking for the ones who have made themselves ready. He is looking for the light. He is inspecting the church body and looking for holiness and righteousness. He is looking for His fruit. Yes, some of us may be able to preach and teach. Some of us may be awesome counselors or administrators. However, never forget that those gifts are temporary and one day they will cease.

Therefore, we must focus on what is most important. As born-again believers, how are we living. Does our life glorify God? What choices are we making on a daily basis? Are we fulfilling our God given purpose? Does our life display the fruit of the Spirit? Do the people we encounter daily witness love, joy, peace, longsuffering, kindness, goodness, faithfulness, gentleness, and self-control?

As born-again believers of Christ, we were all re-born to one day become a bride. It is a part of God's perfect plan and design. The Love that comforts our very soul is returning to embrace His bride. A celebration unlike anything we can ever imagine. It is a glorious moment in time that has been set aside from the very beginning, and it was designed specifically for us. So, my sisters and brothers, are you in preparation mode? Are you excited and filled with zeal about your future? Are you actively striving, working, and preparing for that magnificent moment? Your day; that great wedding day? If not, it is time you get started.

2

A Love that Transforms

"If you love Me, keep My commandments. And I will pray the Father, and He will give you another Helper, that He may abide with you Forever."

—JOHN 14:15–16 (NKJV)

⟡

There is nothing more beautiful than a bride preparing to walk down the aisle to meet her groom. As the door opens the wedding guests take a deep gasp for air when they look upon her beauty as she basks in the glow of that moment. She is breathtakingly beautiful. What is it about that moment that leaves us in awe? Some may think it is the wedding dress. Some may speculate that it must be the makeup. However, I must disagree on both accounts. Now, I do believe that some wedding gowns are incredibly beautiful, and I also must agree that a light application of makeup does sometimes enhance the appearance of our physical beauty. However, this is an outward presentation of the incredible change that is taking place from within. At this moment, the spirit within the bride is glowing because she is being transformed into something new and sacred. She is about to become one with her priest, her provider, and her protector. Therefore, this glow and beauty is the illuminated shine that is manifested from within as a result of her union with her covering.

True love transforms you. You change, you are not the same person. The scripture explains the two shall become one flesh.

> *Therefore shall a man leave his father and his mother; and shall cleave unto his wife: and they shall be one flesh.*
>
> (GENESIS 2:24 KJV)

This is the reason marriage designed by God is special and different. It is a Holy Union that is beautiful, blessed, sacred, committed and filled with sacrifices. From the moment the vows are spoken, physically (to your earthly mate) and spiritually (to Christ), the love you confess should begin to change your mind, body, and soul. Think about it, have you ever been in love? Come on, some of those relationships may not be easy to think about, but I need you to go there with me, just for a moment. Think about that relationship, the one where you gave them your heart, your time, your finances and more than likely your body. You gave them your all. I know you remember. Why do you think you responded that way? Well, it is simple, because that is just a natural response to love.

So, my question to you is does God receive the same response? You love Him also right? Does He have total and complete access to your heart, your time, your finances, and your body? Have you ever made up your mind that you were absolutely determined that you would never do a certain thing again; yet, two weeks later you find yourself indulging in that very same activity. Seriously, at some point in time I know you said to yourself, I am done. I am not doing this anymore. I am changing my ways. I am going to do things differently. You may have said, I am going to stop hanging out in nightclubs and drinking. You may have said I am going to stop smoking and/or using profanity. Prayerfully, at some point you said that you will not have sexual relations again until you are "legally" married. Yet, before you know it, you are back in the same situation.

Now you think, what is wrong with me? You are not alone. We sit in church for worship on Sundays, Bible Study on Wednesdays, prayer meeting, choir rehearsal, missionary meeting, deacon board meeting and so on and so on. Additionally, even though in the year of 2020 the country was in the middle of a Coronavirus pandemic that restricted us from assembling in the physical church building structures. We have not been restricted of the Word of God. We, the body of born-again believers, are the church. And we are blessed and sufficiently equipped to receive sound doctrine via the social media, internet streaming, podcasts, smartphone mobile devices, television, radio, satellite radio, telephonically, and ultimately through the teaching and inspiration of the Holy Spirit during our personal study time. Yet, week after week, we get up from our choice and moment of spiritual impartation and leave the Word of God behind. But as you read this book just know that this message has been specifically designed and packaged for you. The message is simple, clear, and direct. Are you ready? Here, it is ... true love transforms you. Now close your eyes and let the Lord whisper it once more in your spirit ... *true love transforms you.*

We keep messing this "love thing" up and missing the mark, because we (the church) refuse to embrace His design for love and for the church. Our very foundation is to love. But we must learn what that means. The world teaches us that love is all about emotions. When God teaches us, that love is about our actions.

> Jesus said in (John 14:15–17 NRSV), "If you love Me, you will keep My commandments. And I will ask the Father, and He will give you another Advocate, to be with you forever. This is the Spirit of truth, whom the world cannot receive, because it neither sees Him nor knows Him. You know Him, because He abides with you, and He will be in you."

Here, Jesus is giving us truth. He clearly describes the prescription and design for love. Love is a voluntarily submitted life of following Christ's example of holiness and righteousness. Love is about sacrifice, and obedience. Can you really say you love someone if you actively participate in activities that you know would hurt or upset them? Think about it, how would you feel if you were in a relationship with someone who continuously participate in activities that they know hurt you, disrespect you or betray you. Love is a choice. Love is totally choosing to surrender to pleasing the one you Love. When we fail to follow God's design, this is why we continue to end up in hurtful relationships under the pretense of love. This is also why we sometimes continue to participate in unfulfilled activities, groups and gatherings that do not glorify our Lord and Savior in an attempt to "fit-in". We are trying to fill an emptiness or void that is only designed for Christ and the Holy Spirit. Our love for Jesus must come first. That is the first love that will lead and guide you into the arms of the physical being that was strategically designed for your life.

My brothers and sisters, we must accept and understand that the message is not, you should do the best you can. It is not, it is ok, God knows your heart. No, I am sorry but that is not the message God laid on my heart to share with you. This message is for me, you and the entire body of Christ and it is simply this; true love transforms you. Remember, you became a new creation. Our old things have fallen away. Because of our love for Him, God now desires and expects a changed life. A life that chooses to follow His lead and to live by His example.

I know this seems impossible. But, fret not your heart, there is a blessing. He does not put expectations on us without explanation, guidance and assistance. Remember, He loves us, He truly does. As a result, love buckles down and sacrifices right there beside the one they love. Love never leaves you to struggle or suffer alone. If you are in a relationship and never receive the support you desire from your partner, you soon begin to question their love for you. Beloved, we do not have to worry about that with Christ. He is always going to be there for the one He loves. We do not have to blindly walk and figure this journey called life out on our own. He is there to help us, lead us, guide us, and oftentimes carry us through life's trials and tribulations. All we have to do is submit our life in His hands, commit our heart to His word and omit our fleshly desires for His design, destiny, and plan. Then work, watch, wait, and bask in the glory of our transformation into God's image.

> (Romans 12:1–2 NKJV) I beseech you therefore, brethren, by the mercies of God, that you present your bodies a living sacrifice, holy, acceptable to God, which is your reasonable service. And do not be conformed to this world, but be transformed by the renewing of your mind, that you may prove what is that good and acceptable and perfect will of God.

Do you know that according to this scripture, we are either a product of being **conformed** to this world or being **transformed** into the image of Jesus Christ? It is either one or the other, do you know where you stand? The word transformed gives us our English word metamorphosis. Metamorphosis describes the transformation that takes place when a caterpillar transforms into a butterfly. It is a profound change in form from one stage to the next. The caterpillar changes from the caterpillar to the pupa and then from the pupa to the adult butterfly. Although an outward change in appearance and form takes place, the change actually comes from within the life of that incredible organism.

In God's infinite wisdom, the caterpillar is born with the ability to become a butterfly. The butterfly is actually already on the inside of the caterpillar, and as long as the caterpillar eats, the caterpillar's digestive system takes in the nutrients, consumes them, integrates them into its system, which causes it to grow. Then, over time that caterpillar eventually changes its form and becomes a real, genuine butterfly: a beautiful creation that was designed by God. The caterpillar completely transforms into a totally different creation. It is now a butterfly and once this process is complete, it is final. The butterfly never returns to its original form. The butterfly will never be a caterpillar again. The caterpillar's transformation into a butterfly is an extraordinary imagery of what God speaks of in the scriptures concerning the transformation of believers into the image of Christ.

Romans Chapter 12 teaches us what God expects from His people. The chapter starts with Paul saying, "I beseech you therefore, brethren, by the mercies of God ..." (Romans 12:1 KJV). He is actually appealing to the church, not to the world, but appealing to the will of the believer. Paul is letting us know that God calls for His people to make a choice on how we choose to live. His appeal is that we should choose to live for God because of what God has already done for us. Because of His grace and mercy and the mercies He has shown over our lives, and over the lives of our families, such as our children, our parents, our grandparents and great grandparents; the very least we should do is to present our bodies as a living sacrifice. Paul is explaining that this is true and genuine worship.

Worship is our lifestyle. Worship is not simply those ten or fifteen minutes before service where we raise our hands and sing melodious praises. No, my friends, true worship is our everyday choices and decisions. It is where we go, who we hang with, the language we use and the things we choose to participate in. True godly worship means that everything we do is done with the mindset to glorify God. So, Paul is appealing to the will of the believer because it must be a personal choice and a personal decision. No one can force you to serve God. This is why, the appeal calls for us to make a decision on how we chose to live our lives. God will not force us to follow Him or to obey Him. God will never take away our free will to serve Him. So, Paul pleads for believers to freely choose to present their bodies as a "living sacrifice".

Present means to place at one's disposal. It is a call to commit. Paul knew and understood that this is not an easy request. He knows that there will always be a constant battle between the flesh and the spirit.

> *For what I am doing, I do not understand. For what I will to do, that I do not practice; but what I hate, that I do.*
>
> (ROMANS 7:15 NKJV)

Paul knows there is something about our fleshly bodies that can keep us from worshipping God in spirit and in truth. For instance, we must realize and accept the fact that it does not matter how amazing our singing voice may be, if we are constantly and consistently choosing to live a life participating in sinful activities, our life is not worship to God. You may be able to teach like Paul and preach like Peter, but if your lifestyle is raggedy, it is not worship to the Lord.

Paul is pleading with the church to make the decision to be a living sacrifice. A sacrifice in the Old Testament was to bring a live animal to the altar. The animal was then put to death. Its blood was shed and then the animal's flesh was burned on the altar to atone for the sins of the people. The sacrifice came to the altar alive; but it was unable to move because it died on the altar. However, the sacrifice that Paul is speaking of is a little different. Here God is requiring a Living Sacrifice. Paul is asking us to <u>willingly surrender</u> our bodies to the Lord for His use. We are to place our bodies on the altar alive, totally submitted to Him. You see a living sacrifice has the ability to choose to get up and get off the altar when things get tough, yet, because of our love for God, the living sacrifice willingly chooses to stay. Even though things get hard, even though things get painful, even though things get uncomfortable and stressful, our will and desire are to stay, totally committed to surrendering fully to God. We willingly and intentionally choose to lay our bodies down on the altar forever.

To present our body as a living sacrifice is to release control of our entire body, not part of our body but the entire body. We literally should focus and understand that we are giving up control of every part of our body because it all belongs to the Lord. My eyes, ears, hands, feet, heart, and mouth all belong to God. Therefore, I must be careful about the things I choose to watch on television with my eyes, the books I choose to read and the internet searches I choose to conduct, because my eyes belong to God. I must be careful about the music I listen to. My ears belong to God. Think about it? What songs are you allowing to enter those sacred ear canals? Does it glorify God? What about our feet. Where are you allowing God's feet to carry you? Where did your feet take you last weekend or even last night? We must be careful and cautious about where we go. What about our mouth? Are we gossiping and using harsh language? Are we constantly using profanity? Are we telling dirty jokes or even saying hurtful things against other people? Do our hands and fingers glorify God? What are we touching, holding or typing with our hands and fingers? Do our text messages and Facebook/Instagram/twitter/ instant messages glorify God? And we must not forget, but yes, even those precious private parts must be sacrificed and placed on the altar. Are those precious parts protected and set aside to bring God glory? Or is Satan celebrating because he knows that God has no control over our private parts and bodies and that he is the one who really has total control over those areas on a consistent basis.

We are expected to present our entire body as a living sacrifice, holy, and acceptable to God. This sacrifice is the ultimate proof of our love. Nothing says I love you to the Lord but a consecrated, dedicated and holy life. God does not accept anything and everything. I am not quite sure where we get that from, but it is not sound biblical doctrine. Our sacrifice must be alive, holy and pleasing to God. Yet, we are living in a time where holy living is no longer important, required, and rarely preached about. We have "professed Christians" who believe that we can do what we want. Some feel like we can look like the world, dress like the world, and act like the world. However, holy conduct is required in the life of a Christian. Holiness is simply to be set aside for God's use. This person freely chooses to be guided by the principles of the word of God. It is just reasonable and rational behavior as believers to fully dedicate ourselves to God, as a response to what God has already done for us.

> "But now you must be holy
> in everything you do, just as
> God who chose you is holy."
> (I Peter 1:15 NLT)

To conform is to fashion, shape or mold after, to follow a prescribed pattern. As believers we are not to copy the behaviors and customs of the world. We are not to allow the pleasures and pressures of the world to change us. We are to be transformed (changed inwardly) by the renewing of our minds. The mind is the root of our problems. Christians must think differently. If we sit around and think about sinful activities, we will eventually participate in sinful activities. Nevertheless, if we focus our mind to thinking on Godly and right behaviors, the body will follow in obedience. This is the behavior and lifestyle that is well pleasing and satisfying to God. When we confessed and prayed to receive Christ as our Lord and Savior, we were regenerated, or reborn, with God's life to become children of God. We were reborn with the divine life of God living within us. This life transforms us into the image of Christ. But, like the caterpillar, we must stay in the process of transformation by feasting and eating on the Word of God. The Lord wills for us to take Him as our spiritual food. *(John 6:35 NKJV), And Jesus said to them, "I am the bread of life. He who comes to Me shall never hunger, and he who believes in Me shall never thirst."*

When we focus on Christ and His word as our food, more of His elements are added to us and assimilated by us. Then we will eventually undergo a transformation that is not only an outward change, but one that comes from being spiritually nourished where the life of God is operating on the inside. New creatures are developed, and the old man is dead, non-existent. If we truly gave our life to Him, the old life no longer exists. The Holy Spirit transforms our lives, and we will never be the same. As a result, we will soon begin to no longer desire the same things. We will no longer want to have all the same friends or the same activities or pleasures. The Word of God begins to change our mind. It is a changed life, a transformed life. But we have to give our life to Christ for real. We have to die to our flesh for real. We have to present our body as a living sacrifice *for real*.

It is true, the Lord loves us all just as we are. But His love for us is not up for question. It is our love for Him that is questionable. Remember, love and obedience go hand and hand. Jesus is indeed coming back, beloved, but we must remember that He is not coming back for the people He loves; He is coming back for the people who love Him. Jesus is coming back for His bride, the one who loves Him. The one who has made herself ready.

> *"If you [really] love Me, you will keep and obey My commandments."*
>
> (JOHN 14:15 AMP)

A transformed life is a life full of love, beauty, splendor, and filled with the glory of God. Just like the butterfly, it is a life that has been transformed into a new creation. Still, it is an intentional process of a life that has completely decided to submit to the Lord. So, you must ask yourself, what do I need to put on the altar? What part of my body am I holding back from the Lord? What am I holding on to that God has told me to walk away from? My brothers and sisters, He loves you and He is waiting to help you. We do not have to do this alone. Jesus understands our struggles. He knows the strongholds and fleshly desires that we fight with daily. Because of His love for you, He stands at the door and waits for the invitation to step in and rebuke your storm. He is waiting to mold, change, and transform you into His likeness, His bride. The person you were born to be.

3

Blinded by Beauty

"Before I formed thee in the belly, I knew thee; and before thou camest forth out of the womb I sanctified thee, and I ordained thee a prophet unto the nations."

—JEREMIAH 1:5 (KJV)

⁓※⁓

I recently listened to a radio interview of a young female evangelist giving her testimony. This evangelist indicated she had been in the ministry for approximately eighteen years. In the interview, she talked about an experience she encountered while dating a single male pastor. The young lady indicated that she was pursued by this young man after preaching during a Singles' Conference that his church sponsored. She states, she was not interested at first; however, this young pastor soon won her heart. According to this evangelist, the two dated and became "best friends". She asserts that her beau expressed to her that he respected her because he saw something in her that he did not see in other women and that was the fact that she did not want to have sex outside of marriage. Therefore, for approximately a year and a half, they practiced celibacy. He assured her that he was willing to wait for her. The pastor indicated to her that he was so impressed and attracted to her discipline. This young woman felt as though this young man respected her boundaries and that this relationship was "sincere and pure." She asserted that they would pray, fast, read, study, and discuss the word regularly.

Once the young pastor determined that he wanted to be with her long term, he decided to make the announcement to his church body. Afterwards, since the couple lived in two different states, that young pastor decided to move her to his location. He wanted her to move into his home with him; however, she refused, stating, "until we are legally married, I do not want to stay in your house." He respected her position and rented her an apartment not far from his home. He paid for everything. As a result, this young lady did not have any reason to believe that he was not the one. She said that this young man told her that he was going to love her for the rest of her life.

One Friday night after celebrating her birthday, this young man stated, "I want to make you my wife now, so let us take vows." He then pulls out the minister's book that he uses to marry people and he recited his vows first and the evangelist proceeded by reciting her vows. He then stated that they would go to the courthouse on Monday to make it official. That night they consummated the relationship by having sexual intercourse for the first time.

On Monday, when the evangelist asked what time they were going to the courthouse, he responded that they needed to work on some things before we go to the courthouse. This evangelist refused to let it go and reminded the young pastor of Friday's conversation. Yet, her attempts failed as he continued to say things such as "in the Bible they did not do all the courthouse stuff and that it did not matter as long as they took their vows before God". He told her that they were married in the sight of God.

At first the young lady indicated that she did not see it, but soon realized afterwards that this was a very calculated move of events on behalf of this young pastor and that she had been "played."

Wow!!! It appears that this young lady got so caught up on the desire of becoming a wife that she ignored all the signs and red flags. Yearning to get married is a natural and normal desire. However, becoming an "earthly bride" should never come at the expense of aborting, derailing, or delaying our spiritual purpose.

I am sure most of you are wondering, how this young lady could not have seen this coming? Some may even be questioning why God would allow this to happen to a woman who appears to be so committed and dedicated to serving Him. Well, if we are going to be truthful, we need to admit that we have all been there. Everyone reading this book at some point or another got lost in the thrill of fulfilling the pleasures of the flesh, while our purpose lingered dormant within us.

Now, we may not all have all experienced the same type of situation. However, make no mistake, we have all been lost in a moment or caught up in some act of sinful passion. Therefore, at some point, we all must come to the understanding that our fleshly desires will always be at war with our spiritual purpose. I am a firm believer, that in order to overcome the trap of the continuous cycles of failure, we have to be willing to accept responsibility for our actions. We have to come to a place where we make a decision that in order to avoid the pain, embarrassment, and discomfort of rebuilding from a place of shame and brokenness, as a result of succumbing to the deceitfulness or spiritual manipulation of man (male or female). We will have to choose not to ignore the voice, guidance and direction of the Holy Spirit.

> The temptations in your life are no different from what others experience. And God is faithful. He will not allow the temptation to be more than you can stand. When you are tempted, he will show you a way out so that you can endure. (I Corinthians 10:13 NLT)

When we allow our fleshly desires to take control, reason and rationale pick up and completely move out, as our hormones begin to race, and the emotions of the moment begin to take us to a land of darkness and down a road of destruction. We must be willing to step back and pay attention. As believers, the Lord said "… I will never leave you nor forsake you" (Hebrews 13:5 NKJV). Therefore, we need to understand that His Word is there to lead and guide us. We were born for a specific purpose for the Kingdom of God. And the person who God has designed for our life will never fight against, alter, or conflict with that purpose.

Following Christ allows us to clearly see the traps and dangers that were designed for our destruction. We must be careful to stay focused in order to not become blinded by beauty. <u>Blinded</u> by definition means being unable to see, lacking perception, awareness or discernment. Imagine sitting in a room in total darkness with a blindfold covering your eyes. Now, think about how it feels to be awake, yet, in total darkness? Helen Keller, a well-known author, and lecturer was both deaf and blind. She once stated, "the only thing worse than being blind is having sight but no vision".

When we are unable to see, we are incapable of discerning what is in front of us; therefore, we really cannot determine the danger we may or may not be in. When people are physically blind, they always have something around them that they can trust, such as, a person, a seeing eye dog, or a walking cane to help them avoid danger.

Nevertheless, what is even more dangerous than being physically blind is being spiritually blind. Spiritual blindness is more of a choice. It is voluntarily choosing a path of destruction. It is intentionally choosing to walk contrary to the path and design that God has designed for our lives. We do not like the word voluntary because we like to think certain things "just happen." But no, our lifestyles and the choices we make to live in disobedience to the Word of God is what places us on the path of destruction.

When we allow the flesh to control us and when we make intentional decisions to let "ungodly" wants and desires lead us, we eventually become unable to discern reality and truth. We are unable to see the hurt, pain and trouble that are waiting for us because of our choices. King David stood on a balcony looking at a woman named Bathsheba and just lost all sense of reason. (found in II Samuel, chapter 11) He got so caught up in the beauty of that scene that he committed adultery and eventually had Bathsheba's husband killed attempting to hide his sin and weakness. Then there was David's son Amnon. According to the word of God, this young man was so in love with his sister Tamar, that he had to have her, so he raped her and then he did not want anything to do with her (found in II Samuel, chapter 13).

These young men were unable to see the consequences, or the

repercussions of their actions, because they became blinded by the beauty of the moment. Their only focus was that the flesh wanted what the flesh wanted. It is a natural reaction to get caught up for a moment with the physical beauty of the opposite sex. And as I said earlier, if we were all going to be honest, most if not all of us have been there. However, there must come a time when we (you and I) have to get tired of wearing the blinders. Tired of being blinded by beauty, a moment of passion and a temporary moment of pleasure. There must come a time, when we maintain an earnest desire to walk in the light instead of stumbling around in darkness.

We often hear that we are born with purpose. What exactly does that mean? Purpose by definition means the reason for which something is done, created or the reason for which something exists. Born with purpose means that there is a specific reason we each were created. It means that our existence is for a specific reason.

God created us with purpose, and He gives us the direction to find it as long as we are open to seeking Him and listening for His voice. In 2002, Pastor Rick Warren released a bestselling book entitled "Purpose Driven Life." In this book, Pastor Warren clearly explains that discovering our purpose is what defines our lives. Our purpose is filled with passion and results in our greatest fulfilment. Operating in our purpose is the key element to a life that flourishes. It drives us to pursue goals and ultimately live a life of substance and true happiness. The late Pastor Myles Munroe once explained that we were all born to solve a specific problem and that our very existence is to fulfill the need for that particular problem. Therefore, no one's birth is a mistake, we are all necessary.

The Book of Judges introduces a young man who was clearly marked with purpose from his mother's womb.

> Again the Israelites did evil in the eyes of the LORD, so the LORD delivered them into the hands of the Philistines for forty years. A certain man of Zorah, named Manoah, from the clan of the Danites, had a wife who was childless, unable to give birth. The angel of the LORD appeared to her and said, "You

are barren and childless, but you are going to become pregnant and give birth to a son. Now see to it that you drink no wine or other fermented drink and that you do not eat anything unclean. You will become pregnant and have a son whose head is never to be touched by a razor because the boy is to be a Nazarite, dedicated to God from the womb. He will take the lead in delivering Israel from the hands of the Philistines." Then the woman went to her husband and told him, "A man of God came to me. He looked like an angel of God, very awesome. I didn't ask him where he came from, and he didn't tell me his name. But he said to me, 'You will become pregnant and have a son. Now then, drink no wine or other fermented drink and do not eat anything unclean, because the boy will be a Nazarite of God from the womb until the day of his death.' (Judges13:1–7 NLT)

As promised, this young woman later gave birth to a son and she named him Samson. The child that she had prayed for, the answer to her prayers was now resting peacefully in her arms. This child was chosen by God from the womb to be a Nazarite. A Nazarite is an Israelite who is consecrated by vow to the service of God. This simply means he was separated, set aside, and dedicated to God and for God's use. The sign of this commitment was that Samson (1) was not to drink wine or any intoxicated drink (2) was not allowed to touch anything dead and (3) no razor was to ever come upon his head.

Samson was anointed by the Spirit of God. He was specifically chosen to take the lead in delivering Israel out of the hands of the Philistines. He was born with purpose. There was something incredibly special and supernatural about this young man's presence and his strength. He once slew 1000 Philistines in one day and killed a lion with his bare hands. When you think about Samson's characteristics, it is hard to imagine him as just a man. Yet, that is exactly what he was. He was a man chosen and appointed for a specific assignment, just like you and me. And just like you and me, Samson was faced with dealing with the battle between the flesh and the spirit.

Life happened, and Samson was soon confronted with making choices and decisions. Samson had to decide on whether he was going to stay committed to His God and his purpose or yield to the temptations of the flesh.

The scriptures explain that Samson fell in love with a Philistine woman named Delilah. The rulers of the Philistines tasked Delilah to entice Samson to divulge the secret of his strength. As Samson rested in her lap, Delilah repeatedly nagged Samson to tell her the secret. After being tormented repeatedly by Delilah's nagging, Samson finally confessed to Delilah that his hair has never been cut because he was dedicated to God as a Nazirite from birth. He told her that if his hair were shaved that his strength would leave him, and he would be as weak as everyone else. Delilah shared this information with the Philistines. Samson's hair was shaven, and the Philistines paid Delilah 1100 pieces of silver for her betrayal against Samson. Samson was later awakened as the Philistines came in to capture him. Samson lunged to break loose but did not realize that the Lord had left him. (found in Judges 16)

What are some practical points that we learn from the story of Samson?

1. We are all chosen and birthed with purpose!

Samson's purpose was to lead God's people out of the hands of the Philistines. Samson was specifically chosen from conception. How amazing is that? What a privilege it is to be chosen by God for a specific reason and purpose. But do you realize that God did not stop with Samson. We were all born with purpose. What is your purpose? Are you willingly fulfilling your purpose or are you allowing the pleasures of life to suppress your purpose?

2. Do not ignore God's rules and boundaries!

Rules and boundaries were designed and created for our protection. God created laws and boundaries for the life of believers.

And although we are no longer under the Law, we still have rules, guidelines, instructions and expectations under Grace. Jesus did not come to do away with the law, He came to fulfill it. He came to teach us how to love. Jesus said ..."You shall love the LORD your God with all your heart, with all your soul, and with all your mind.' This is the first and great commandment. And the second is like it: 'You shall love your neighbor as yourself.' On these two commandments hang all the Law and the Prophets." (Matthew 22:37-40 NKJV) When we think about it, if we live according to those two standards the other eight will take care of themselves. A man cannot love his neighbor while sleeping with his neighbor's wife. Children cannot genuinely love the Lord and disrespect their mother and father. We as Christians must accept the fact that we have boundaries and guidelines. We cannot choose to live our lives doing what we want. We each must make the decision that *our purpose is more important than our pleasure.* Samson was on assignment. He had a specific purpose, yet he chose to ignore God's voice and instructions. He stepped outside of God's will for his life for his own pleasure and fulfillment. What boundaries are you currently ignoring? How is your purpose suffering because of your desire to feed your flesh?

3. Learn from the mistakes we make!

Yes, Samson messed up. However, the reality is, so have we. How many times do we continue to do the same things over and over? During their romantic interactions, Delilah states to Samson, "how can you say, 'I love you,' when you won't confide in me? This is the third time you have made a fool of me and haven't told me the secret of your great strength." (Judges 16:15 NIV). This is the third time that Delilah is attempting to betray Samson and he is still choosing to spend intimate quality time with her. He still chooses to trust her when she has repeatedly shown herself untrustworthy. What will it take for us to learn our lesson? Why do we continue to do the same thing over and over and over again? We oftentimes relive the same experiences of pain and brokenness because we refuse to accept fault and make a decision to change directions. Three times!!! Why would

Samson choose to stay? Why would he choose to let his guard down when she had already displayed that she could not be trusted? Or was it that Samson just could not see the truth because he was blinded by beauty. Beloved, the sad reality is that as long as we are operating outside the will of God, we subject ourselves to having to stumble around in darkness. When the flesh has primary control over our thoughts, words, and deeds, we are not allowing any room for the leading of the Holy Spirit. Jesus tells us *"Behold, I stand at the door and knock. If anyone hears My voice and opens the door, I will come in to him and dine with him, and he with Me." (Revelation 3:20 NKJV)*

Jesus will never force us to follow Him. That is a free-will choice we must make. We rarely talk about this, but Samson had already partaken in ungodly relationships. Delilah was not the first. This is why we must be willing to totally surrender to the leading of the Holy Spirit. When God delivers us from a situation, never look back. Repent, and move forward in a different direction. We must learn to turn away from the things that are not pleasing to our Lord and Savior.

Sleeping with Delilah was literally sleeping with the enemy. Delilah pestered him until he became so angry and annoyed that he gave in and gave up the most precious part of his soul, his heart. We have to be careful who we give our heart to. It is precious, it is valuable, it is delicate, and it belongs to the Lord. Therefore, He is the only One who has a right to give it away. This is why we have to be careful with whom we associate. Why spend time entertaining someone that cannot be trusted? If you find yourself constantly checking their phone, stalking them on social media and questioning their every move, should you still be entertaining that relationship? How can a person expect to hear from God when they are constantly walking around angry, annoyed, and irritated? Remember, God will not force Himself into our heart and soul. We need a peaceful spirit in order to hear the guidance and counsel of the Holy Spirit. Like Samson, many of us refuse to learn from our mistakes. Samson did not learn that lesson until it was too late. His fleshly desires were continuously winning the battle over his spiritual purpose. This happened repeatedly; until one day the Philistines captured him and plucked out his eyes. Samson was seized and blinded because he chose to focus on fulfilling temporary pleasures instead of embracing his permanent purpose. What lessons are we refusing to learn from the mistakes we have made?

4.   Do not allow sinful activities to separate us from God!

Samson allowed sin to separate him from God. Samson's blindness represents the fact that sin will deceive you. When we choose to continue to intentionally live a life of sin, we will ultimately lose our spiritual sight. The more we step outside the boundaries the easier it becomes and the more natural it becomes to live contrary to the Word of God. Samson went to the vineyard, yet he was not supposed to touch anything from the vine. One could question, why was he there. Samson ate honey out of the lion's carcass, when he was not supposed to touch anything unclean. And the last of the Nazarite vow that he had not broken was to keep a razor from touching his hair, yet he allowed his fleshly hormones to lure him into breaking that one. Samson kept on and on until God left him. But the saddest part about it was that he did not even realize it.

> Then she called, Samson, the Philistines are upon you!
> He awoke from his sleep and thought, I'll go out as
> before and shake myself free. But he did not know that
> the LORD had left him. (Judges 16:20 NIV)

Samson lived in compromise for so long that he thought it would never make a difference in his strength and anointing. Samson's strength was not only about his hair, it was in his relationship with God. We cannot stay in "right" relationship with God and do what we want to do. Samson's consequence to his life of disobedience was physical blindness. His eyes were plucked out by the Philistines. However, my desire is for us not to be too hard on Samson because of the choices he made, but for us to learn from Samson and his choices. Because truthfully, thousands of years later, we are still making the same mistakes Samson made.

Several years ago, a young woman named Tina was also blinded by the beauty of the moment. One day out of the blue she received a message from a certain young man very similar to this ... I am not one for beating around the bush. I was telling a friend that I would love the opportunity to wine and dine you. Can I take you out? I am sure you are going to say yes, LOL. So, check your calendar and see when you can fit me into your busy schedule. You are a very attractive woman, and I also love the fact that you are a woman of character and a Christian. So, don't keep me waiting. I am looking forward to finally meeting you.

This message completely caught Tina off guard, but truthfully, she was totally flattered. This particular young man had sparked an interest with Tina over ten years previously. At that time, He was also apparently interested, but for whatever reason he felt as though Tina ignored him. So approximately ten years later he decided to try once more. Tina became totally caught up in her internal desire for a relationship that she began to overlook some noticeably clear warning signs. In the beginning the young man seemed to be everything she wanted, desired, and had asked God for. He was a tall, handsome, professional black man. But most importantly, he was a Christian. Seriously, on the surface, this man had it all. What more can a girl ask for?

Then reality hit Tina hard in the face. She was blinded by beauty. You see, she prayed to God as she always did with any potential relationship and God answered. Tina knew it was God because she never had an inner peace within her spirit that this was the right situation. Yet, she chose to continue to communicate and flirt with this young man through social media, knowing it was not right, yet hoping that her interpretation of what she was feeling within was wrong. As a result, her heart became attached to a situation that the Lord had not approved of.

Tina was blessed that God stepped in and blocked the relationship from officially connecting. Yes, God blocked it!! And even though she had to deal with the internal emotions of attraction and infatuation, the Lord protected her from physically meeting, developing, and falling deeply in love with a man who was not assigned to her destiny.

Because of Tina's failure to take heed to the voice of God immediately, she had to suffer through the pain of disappointment, the feeling of hurt and the struggle of letting go.

Beloved, the Father, the Son and the Holy Spirit are always there to lead and guide us. However, we must be willing to listen. Now please do not misunderstand me. Just because God said no to that particular union between Tina and the young man, does not mean that that particular young man cannot make some woman a wonderful husband. I believe with the help of the Lord; we are all capable to being fabulous mates and incredible blessings. But we have to be willing to listen for God's voice and willing to follow His lead. And as a friend of mine often reminds me, we must always remember that God's timing is always perfect. No matter how disappointing or painful some situations may be, we must learn to trust the Lord's blueprint for our life. There is always a reason and a purpose behind God's decisions.

I praise God for Jesus. He chose to come as the perfect Nazarite, to deliver us from the bondage of blindness. He came so that we can have light. He said in His Word that, *"Thy word is a lamp unto my feet, and a light unto my path." (Psalm 119:105 KJV)* We do not have to live in darkness. We do not have to travel down a road of destruction. We do not have to succumb to the desires of our flesh. He is truly able to keep us from falling.

Jesus is our light in this dark and dangerous world. He will show up and shine the light on any situation or any subject that may be suspect. I thank God that He loves us just that much. We do not have to worry about being mistreated and deceived as long as we are willing to follow His lead. Trust the God that indwells within your spirit, He loves you. Embrace Him, focus on His love, walk in your purpose, and let His love lead you into the arms of the person that He has designed specifically for you.

4

Maximize the Moment

"Watch therefore, for you know neither the day nor
the hour in which the Son of Man is coming."

—MATTHEW 25:13 (NKJV)

Now that we have embraced the fact that we are the Bride of Christ and born with purpose, how do we as single Christians deal with the constant physical and internal desire to become an earthly husband or wife? Where is our life partner, our constant companion? Where is the love, passion, romance, and sexual intimacy that God designed and approved for our life? Where is that one special person to share life's ups and downs, the good and the bad, the sickness and health? You know, the one that every now and then upsets you, but overall brings you so much joy and happiness, just to share your life with. Lord, where is our "until death do, we part"?

Trust me, many singles feel the same way. Let me take a moment to get a little personal. There are times while lying in bed that the silence blankets my room in the stillness of the night and peace is far from me. I would lie there, desperately wishing for sleep and serenity for I know it is the only way to erase the thoughts and desires for intimacy that is raging within the depths of my soul. I wrestle, fight, and consistently ask; what can I do to get this longing to stop haunting me? What will it take to make it go away? The tears begin to flow uncontrollably as the scripture "Then the LORD God said, "It is not good for the man to be alone. I will make a helper who is just right for him." (Genesis 2:18 NLT), replays over, and over again in my head. As I lie there in the midst of such anguish, I cry out in distress and wonder why God has not answered my most earnest prayer and desire.

Come on, I live day after day, week after week, and year after year, spending time with family and friends, faithfully working and serving in the church as I observe couples and families interacting and enjoying the festivities and events of life. Therefore, surely it should be expected that I would also desire earthly companionship, and love. It does not make sense. Why would God not have a special someone for me? Well, I can firmly testify that in the midst of my low moments, God is always faithful!! In the midst of the pain, struggle, tears and loneliness, His soft still voice whispers, *"Peace, be still"* (*Mark 4:39* KJV). Beloved, please know and understand that there has never been a time when God has not been powerful enough to speak to the storm that was raging within my spirit. There has never been an instance when His Word has not been strong enough to calm the emotions that seemed to have overpowered me by force. There has never been a situation too enormous that the blood He shed on Calvary could not heal. Therefore, there is no emotional storm within you that is too powerful for Him to control.

So, trust me, we are truly on this journey together; therefore, let us walk it out step by step. As a single Christian, do you realize that your "Singleness" is a ministry? I do not believe we really ever focus on that. Yes, single Christians have an assignment from God that is so much more important than the countless hours, days, weeks, months, and years we spend focusing on finding our future mate. Now, I do believe as believers, if it is God's will for your life, that there is indeed a special someone waiting for you. But we must remember that the number one goal of our life is to fulfil God's purpose. We cannot become so caught up in dating, marrying, and having children that we miss God's primary plan and design for our lives. We must continue to stay focused, motivated, and actively preparing for our destiny.

Down through the years our ancestors, our pastors, our friends, our communities, and our parents taught us that marriage is a person's ultimate goal in life. That message was constant and consistent. This oftentimes led to a negative stigma on singleness as shame, disgrace, and dishonor that many people battle with day in and day out. However, I believe our attitudes regarding marriage has somewhat "Shifted", but I am not quite sure if it has shifted for the better. Some statistical data indicates that back in 1950, 80% of American adults were married; however, today's data shows that over half of American adults are single. Now, I am not here to denounce marriage, because I truly believe God created and designed marriage to be an incredible earthly example of Christ's love and relationship with the church. Therefore, my intent is not to paint a negative picture about marriage. However, I am here to erase and reject the negative stain/stigma that has been attached to singleness.

> *"Sometimes I wish everyone were single like me-a simpler life in many ways! But celibacy is not for everyone any more than marriage is. God gives the gift of the single life to some, the gift of the married life to others."*
>
> (I CORINTHIANS 7:7 MESSAGE)

I Corinthians, Chapter 7 teaches that Marriage is a covenant to be united and to be one flesh, between a male and a female. This teaching includes that sexual intimacy is only to be shared within the compounds of that union between that husband and that wife. However, also in Chapter 7 Paul describes singleness as a gift. Even though Paul is teaching on marriage, he says, "I wish that all of you were as I am." At that time, Paul was single, and he identifies it as a gift from God. He asserts that some have the gift of singleness and others have the gift of marriage. Paul explains that because of the gift of singleness, Christians Singles are to be applauded and highly-admired for embracing this gift during the season of singleness, because as singles, we have more time to devout to serving the Lord. So, my single sisters and brothers, this is our time to "Maximize the Moment" in our present state.

Maximize means to make the best use of, to make as great as possible. Moment is the present time. So how do we make the best use of this present time in our current state? How can we be productive, encouraging, and a blessing to the Kingdom of God as a single Christian? How can we be content, and continue to bear fruit when we are "currently" in a situation that we do not necessarily desire to be in? We want to be married, and God knows that. However, right now, the Lord's gift to us is singleness. So, we must be content in that. We must be thankful and satisfied with that. Contentment is a decision not a feeling. It is a determination to be satisfied with the gift that God has given you.

If God is ultimately in charge, as singles we need to remember that we are exactly where God wants us to be. We waste so much time struggling and questioning why we are single, how long are we going to be single, and what am I doing wrong that results in my continued singleness. Well, the bottom line is this. If we are following God and obeying His voice, we do not have to worry, we are exactly where God desires us to be. We have purpose, value, and need, in this moment, in our current state. Now, what are you doing with your gift of singleness?

Take a moment to think back to a time when you were blessed to own a brand-new automobile. You knew without a shadow of doubt that it was a gift from God. Think about that moment when the keys were placed in your hands. How excited, thankful, and grateful you were at that moment. But what if you never actually drove the automobile? You had the keys in your hands, the vehicle was in your possession, you had the authority to use it, you had a license to drive it, you had insurance to cover it, and you had the knowledge and skill set to operate it; yet you never got in the vehicle to drive it. You just let it sit there day after day. People see this gift every day parked in the open. It is visible, it is beautiful, but no one truly knows its value or its worth.

This vehicle has all the features, such as, GPS, Bluetooth, forward collision warning, Android Auto/Apple Car Play, Keyless entry, heated seats, and WIFI Hotspot. It is safe, reliable, and economical. This automobile has everything you need, yet it blesses no one because it is parked. Therefore, this gift is unused, and not fulfilling the purpose that it was designed and created to fulfil. Well, beloved, your singleness is also a gift from God. Now, the question becomes, are you thankful for your gift of singleness and allowing it to fulfill its purpose? Or is your gift parked, un-used, un-fulfilled, un-appreciated, and under-valued? Are you constantly crying out to God that you do not want or appreciate His gift? Are you operating as an un-used and un-purposeful single; or are you content in your current state and intentional about your service for God, fulfilling your purpose, and operating in your gifts?

As a single individual, I have learned to embrace this moment. I choose to serve God and operate in my gift. But I also choose to travel when I want to travel, cook when and if I desire to cook, and shop when I choose to shop. All these types of things will be altered a little when I marry. Yes, many of us will one day get married, but for now, for this moment of singleness, we need to recognize it as the gift that it is. This is the time to serve God, serve man, walk in love, and enjoy life. This is our time to embrace our gift, maximize this moment and prepare for our destiny to one day become a husband or wife.

Do you remember the parable of the ten virgins? The Bridegroom came when it was least expected. This is why we must stay focused and be prepared. Many times, when it seems as though God is not hearing our prayers or in most cases we feel as though He is taking too long to answer our prayers, we get complacent, or we just get tired of waiting. We decide that we are going to take matters into our own hands. This is when things get dangerous. Ladies, this is when we make up in our minds that "having a piece of man is better than having no man at all." And fellows, this is when you decide to date a woman that is not your future, just your right now. Beloved, we cannot lose focus, we cannot lose the excitement, and we cannot lose the zeal to trust God and walk in our purpose. We must make our mind up that we will fight to maintain the passion for our "First love" and that we will stay committed to our Heavenly calling. As believers we should always remember that God will come through for us. No matter how long it takes, never lose faith, and never forget that God's timing is truly always perfect.

> Then the kingdom of heaven shall be likened to ten virgins who took their lamps and went out to meet the bridegroom. Now five of them were wise, and five were foolish. Those who were foolish took their lamps and took no oil with them, but the wise took oil in their vessels with their lamps. But while the bridegroom was delayed, they all slumbered and slept. "And at midnight a cry was heard: 'Behold, the bridegroom is coming; go out to meet him!' Then all those virgins arose and trimmed their lamps. And the foolish said to the wise, 'Give us some of your oil, for our lamps are going out.' But the wise answered, saying, 'No, lest there should not be enough for us and you; but go rather to those who sell, and buy for yourselves.' And while they went to buy, the bridegroom came, and those who were ready went in with him to the wedding; and the door was shut. "Afterward the other virgins came also, saying, 'Lord, Lord, open to us!' But he answered and said, 'Assuredly, I say to you, I do not know you.' Watch therefore, for you know neither the day nor the hour in which the Son of Man is coming. (Matthew 25:1–13 NKJV)

In this set of scriptures, the virgins represent followers of Christ. They represent the church members. Therefore you, me and the entire church body will fall under one of the two categories; we are either wise or foolish. In this particular parable, Jesus differentiates between two distinct classes of believers. The Bridegroom (Christ) will return for His Bride (Church): the one who has prepared herself and fulfilled her purpose by spreading the "good news" which is the Gospel of Christ.

> In Matthew 28:19–20 NLT, the Great Commission commands, Therefore, go and make disciples of all the nations, baptizing them in the name of the Father and the Son and the Holy Spirit. Teach these new disciples to obey all the commands I have given you. And be sure of this: I am with you always, even to the end of the age.

As believers, we have an assignment. And we must remember that our assignment from the Lord comes before our physical desires. We are charged with the responsibility to teach the good news of Jesus Christ to all nations.

Jesus taught in parables regularly during His three-year teaching ministry. A parable is a realistic story that has a spiritual lesson. In the parable of the ten virgins, the lamp represents the word of God, the oil represents the Holy Spirit, the vessels holding the extra oil represent our hearts, the midnight hour represents spiritual darkness, and the wedding represents a covenant union between the Bridegroom and His followers (the church).

Every member of the local churches, male and female, are represented in one of the two groups. Let us look closely at this parable. They are all professed believers. They are all virgins, and they all have lamps. On the surface they all look alike. All ten virgins heard the good news (knew about Christ), they all appear to have accepted Christ and they all confessed to be watching and waiting for His return. Suddenly, when they least expect it, they heard a loud cry that the Bridegroom is on His way. They jumped up and begin to prepare their lamps.

This is when the differences between the two groups begin to surface. As they begin to light their lamps the five foolish virgins discover that they did not have enough oil. As their lamps begin to burn out, they noticed that the five wise virgins were well prepared and had extra oil for their lamps. The foolish virgins appealed to the wise virgins to share their supply. But the wise refused and directed them to go to the market to buy the oil that they needed. Was this a selfish response from the wise virgins? Does their response seem to contradict the foundational teaching we often receive, which is to love and help those in need? Well, before you answer, think about what the oil represents. Remember the oil represents the Holy Spirit. Can we (the church body) provide Oil to others if requested? No, we do not have that power. We can only teach, lead and direct others to the source and the supplier of the oil. That is what the wise virgins did. The Holy Spirit is one thing we cannot share. Only the Lord can give the gift of the Holy Spirit.

Have you ever failed to properly prepare? Maybe it was a test or an assignment that you decided you would just cram for or improvise. The day soon came when it was time for you to perform? At that moment, you recognized your lack of preparedness and realized that there was no one around to help you. As you stood there faced with the uncertainty of the outcome you understood your shortcoming and knew there was not enough time for anyone to share their knowledge with you. But most importantly, you suddenly realized that it was too late for you to properly prepare. Consequently, like the five foolish virgins, you were unprepared for a very important moment and/or event. The sad truth is there is a time of preparation and a time when the market will be closed. It was midnight, what are the chances that the market for the oil would still be open. Understand, there will surely be a moment in time when the preparation period will expire, and the Bridegroom will permanently close the door. The five foolish virgins knocked on the door, but the Bridegroom refused to open the door because He did not know them. Can you imagine that? How devastating would it be for Jesus to say to you, "I do not know you"? They were all holding the Word (the lamps), yet Jesus states to the five foolish virgins that He did not know them.

While you wait, are you preparing to be a bride? The five foolish virgins did not use the time they had been allotted wisely. They failed to fulfill their calling, to wait with purpose and to develop a relationship with Christ. The five foolish virgins knew of Him, but they did not know Him, because the Holy Spirit was not in them. Remember, they had no oil. Man may not be able to tell the difference, but God knows the difference because He can clearly see our heart. Christ will know His bride when He sees her. He knows the one who has made herself ready. He knows the one who has on the robe of righteousness. She is not perfect; but she is committed, because she made the decision to be prepared.

The wise virgins had the Holy Spirit which indicates they loved God with all their heart. This is what separates the wise from the foolish. If you do not have the Spirit of Christ within you, you do not belong to Him. "But you are not in the flesh but in the Spirit, if indeed the Spirit of God dwells in you. Now if anyone does not have the Spirit of Christ, he is not His." (Romans 8:9 NKJV). Beloved, as we wait, let us wait wisely. We must be careful not to be so caught up on when we will meet "Mister or Misses" right, that we are left behind by failing to prepare and choosing to live in spiritual darkness without the light of Christ.

5

Living Single

Then the Lord God said, "It is not good for the man to be alone. I will make a helper who is just right for him."
—GENESIS 2:18 (NLT).

⌑⧝⧝⌑

A few years ago, I was told about a young woman who agreed to live with her boyfriend prior to marriage. This couple had been living together for a while; therefore, they did all the normal things that couples do. You know day after day, week after week, month after month, year after year, they woke up together, went to work, came home, cleaned, cooked, paid bills, and went back to bed ...... together. In her mind, life was wonderful, everything was "peaches and cream," or so she thought. Well, one Saturday morning, the day started out like any other. The couple woke up together, got out of bed and prepared to start their day. There was nothing out of the ordinary, no tension, no arguing, just a normal day. The young man told "his lady" that he had a couple of errands to run. He said his good-bye, kissed her, and told her that he will see her a little later. However, little did she know; that this particular Saturday, was actually his wedding day. Yes, that is right. This man got out of bed with her that morning, went to a local church, stood, and married another woman.

As single Christians, it is important to remember that while dating, we must be led by the Spirit, which means that our lives should line up with the scriptures. We are men and women of purpose. As we discussed earlier, purpose is the reason for which we were created. And that reason is ultimately to glorify God with our life. We cannot glorify God with our life by choosing to live in disobedience to His word. Because of our love for Christ, we must be determined to follow scriptures, walk in the Spirit, and operate in our purpose; even when dating. Beloved, we must be determined to not give in to the emotional roller coaster that has completely overpowered our bodies. It is imperative that we deny our flesh if we desire to please the Lord. The young lady mentioned in the beginning of this chapter was severely emotionally hurt. However, she chose to ignore the Lord's design for love and relationships by putting her love and trust in a man who did not deserve it before putting her love and trust in the Lord. As a result, she was left with an emotional scar that will be very difficult to overcome. Unfortunately, this young sister is not alone. There are many professed "Christians" who continue to live a life led by the flesh and not by the Spirit of God. God's word, standards and principles were designed to protect us. But we must accept, embrace, and follow them. Yes, there will be times when pain and discomfort will show up at our doorsteps even when we are living within God's will and design for our lives. But the blow from the pain seems so much easier to handle due to the peace that comes from God when you are living within His will. "And the peace of God, which transcends all understanding, will guard your hearts and your minds in Christ Jesus." (Philippians 4:7 NIV)

In the Book of Genesis, the first relationship is recorded between Adam and Eve. As singles we find great comfort in reading and believing the scripture God spoke after He created Adam and later Eve as Adam's helper. The scripture states, "Then the LORD God said, "It is not good for the man to be alone. I will make a helper who is just right for him." (Genesis 2:18 NLT). Although this scripture is indeed promising and comforting, there are specific instructions given to Adam in previous scriptures that are important, critical, and often overlooked. God specifically spoke to Adam and gave him specific instructions before He decided to bring a woman into his life. So, I truly believe that God also intends for specific things to be in order in a man's life before he should begin to entertain the idea of engaging in a relationship with a woman.

> Then the Lord God took the man and put him in the garden of Eden to tend and keep it. And the Lord God commanded the man, saying, "Of every tree of the garden you may freely eat; but of the tree of the knowledge of good and evil you shall not eat, for in the day that you eat of it you shall surely die." And the Lord God said, "It is not good that man should be alone; I will make him a helper comparable to him. (Genesis 2:15–18 NKJV)

In the scriptures, God first took the man and placed him in the Garden of Eden where he lived in the presence of God. It was the place where Adam communed with God. I can only imagine that it was a place filled with love, peace, splendor, and beauty. It was the place that God created for Adam to live in peaceful innocence as he reaped the fruits of the Earth. Adam was placed in the garden and instructed to tend the garden. This basically means to work the garden and cultivate it. Work has always been a part of man's perfect existence. Before sin conquered man and before God created woman, God commanded that man work. Therefore, one can argue that a man who is not working, either by choice or by force is a man that is unfulfilled.

Unfulfilled simply means unsatisfied, not having achieved one's desires or full potential. Hence my sisters, you must ask yourself, can an unfulfilled man bring peace and harmony to a relationship? Please note, that men who have reached retirement status and not currently working does not fall within this particular category. Retired men have positioned themselves to still be able to fulfill their obligations of being providers of the household because they continue to have income flowing into the home. Therefore, the principle that we must keep in mind and understand is that God has equipped men with the ability to work in order to be able to provide for their household. The scripture goes on to require man to keep the garden. This means that man was charged with being a protector. From creation, God instilled in man the capabilities to protect what God has blessed him with. And Lastly, God gave Adam a command: which is the Word. God spoke and commanded man to not eat from the tree of knowledge of good and evil or he would surely die.

After the creation of man and specific instructions that God spoke regarding man's responsibilities, it was then that God stated, *"It is not good for the man to be alone."* (Genesis 2:18 NLT) Therefore, it appears that God's order of instructions to men are specific and deliberate. God placed Adam in His presence, gave him the Word, gave him a job, and provided him with the capabilities and skillset to protect his blessings, before He blessed him with a woman. According to this text, it is after this order that a man is prepared and ready to take a wife. A Christian's life is about preparation and process. We will acknowledge and accept the fact that in order to become a physician, attorney, police officer, nurse, fire fighter, or musician, that it takes education, training, and preparation. We understand that this is required and necessary. Yet, we fail to train and prepare for one of the most significant roles that we as humans can hold, which is the role of a husband or wife.

> *Delight thyself also in the Lord:*
> *and he shall give thee the*
> *desires of thine heart.*
>
> (PSALM 37:4 KJV)

The dating process can be a substantial part of this preparation period even though for many this process can be extremely stressful. The dating scene has many single Christians losing hope on any chance of a Godly relationship. This contradicts who we are. We are people of hope. Therefore, we must continue to trust Jesus with His plan for our life. We must trust that when we find delight and enjoyment in serving the Lord that He will respond by giving us the desires of our heart (Psalm 37:4 paraphrased). We should encourage ourselves into believing that if it is God's will, He will bring that one special person in our life who is just as committed to walking in the Spirit as we are. We need to tell ourselves to not give up or to lose hope. Even when there are times when we feel as though there is no hope. Trust me, I feel you; I really am walking through this thing with you. It is in these moments that I begin to reflect and meditate on His Word. It is in these moments that I learn and understand that His Word teaches in *(Psalm 84:11 NLT) "For the LORD God is our sun and our shield. He gives us grace and glory. The LORD will withhold no good thing from those who do what is right."* Exhaling, I choose to trust Him and His word. Even when it does not look like it, I choose to continue to stand on His word, walk by faith and trust His plan.

What does it mean to date under God's plan and design? Is dating even in the Bible?

"Dating" may not specifically be mentioned in the Bible. Probably because in the biblical times the concept of dating did not exist. During the biblical times, an unmarried male and female did not really socialize, gather, or interact alone with each other in the public. Even though the Bible does not speak specifically about dating, the Bible does give great detail and guidance about relationships, principles and maintaining godly standards; and I do believe that dating is a critical step in getting to know people. As Christians, born again believers, we cannot date like the world. Thus, using scriptures, Godly wisdom, and the counsel of the Holy Spirit as our directive helps us to establish a strong foundation.

When dating, always remember that our primary purpose in life is to serve God. So, all we do should ultimately glorify God. So, as we date, we must keep that in mind. Dating is a part of our preparation period. It is a time to allow God to teach us how to become Godly wives and Godly husbands. It is a time used to seek and gather information, to determine if you and this particular person are traveling along the same path. This is the time used to learn specific and relevant information regarding the person you are dating. This is the time to learn the person's character, goals, beliefs, and habits. This is not to say that the person we are searching/waiting for is perfect, because there is only one perfect person that walked the earth and His name is Jesus, who is now sitting on the right side of God interceding on our behalf. Therefore, our earthly mate will be imperfect, just as we are. However, compatibility is crucial and critical in successful relationships. "Can two people walk together without agreeing on the direction?" (Amos 3:3 NLT)

> *"So whether you eat or drink,*
> *or whatever you do, do it all*
> *for the glory of God."*
>
> (I CORINTHIANS 10:31 NIV)

We cannot even walk with God, a perfect Being, unless we agree to follow His direction. Our intimate, peaceful and fulfilling relationship with Christ rests on our decision to come into agreement with Him. The same principal is expected in order to establish intimate, peaceful and fulfilling earthly relationships. We must be in agreement to travel in the same direction. I am not saying that you will always agree on everything, but I am saying that if you plan on living in peace and joy, it is highly recommended that you connect with an individual that shares and supports your core beliefs, values, and principles.

Therefore, when the Lord decides that it is your season to date, walk in your season with pride and purpose and never forget who you are. The Lord loves you and you are precious in His sight. Focus on that. Most importantly, always remember that we are people of hope, so when you date, always date with hope. As I focused on the word hope that the Lord dropped in my spirit, I begin to see that as I date, I should always keep <u>Him</u> first, be <u>Observant</u> of things around me, live within the <u>Principles</u> of His word, and <u>Expect</u> good things to happen to me, because He will keep no good thing from me.

"For I know the plans I have for you," declares the Lord, "plans to prosper you and not harm you, plans to give you hope and a future." (Jeremiah 29:11 NIV). The Lord knows and understands that we sometimes struggle with believing and holding onto hope. So, when we need encouragement,

we must make a habit of seeking the scriptures for comfort and hope. We all need to be reminded that the Father, Son, Holy Spirit and Word of God offer hope for our daily lives. You may not realize it, but God has a plan for your life. Trust Him and walk in that plan. Do not allow anyone to detour you from His path for your life. The Lord is the head of our lives and the owner of our bodies. He has the right to direct and control our paths.

We often look for step-by-step books, guides, and self-help manuals that are loaded with "do's and don'ts" on finding the perfect mate. But there is no manual or guide that should out rank the hope in God's design for our lives. He is our constant companion, guide, and director. Yet, He will not force us to rest our love, faith and hope in Him. He will not fight for your time and attention. The scriptures teach that He stands at the door and knocks as He patiently waits for an invitation into our heart. We can trust Him with every fiber of our being. So, as you read relationship books, guides, and manuals, make sure that they lead you to the path designed by Christ. There is no book that should hold more power or give you more direction for your life than the Bible, and that includes this book. Trust me, I am thankful and grateful to God that you chose to read what I believe God is leading me to share with the world. Still, I pray that you are seeking the Holy Spirit for revelation and truth as you read.

His Word (the Holy Bible) is our final authority. There is nothing anyone should say to you for guidance that contradicts God's scriptures. This reminds me of a moment in time many years ago. I was approximately thirty-eight years old at the time, and for a woman who desperately desired to give birth, it was clear to everyone looking that "my clock was ticking" and I was running out of time. Well, one day, an older female Christian advised me to go ahead, hook up with a man so I could give birth. Her instructions were that you do not have to have a husband in order to have a baby. You need to go ahead before it is too late. Even though her statement was accurate because we all know you do not need a husband in order to give birth. I kindly responded and asked her if this is what God directed her to share with me. Beloved, please remember to never embrace advice or guidance that contradicts the Word of God. Even when people mean well and have good intentions, our lives should be led by the guidance and direction of the Holy Spirit. Yes, God can take our mistakes and work them out for our good. But that should never be our strategic plan and goal. Our goal should be to always follow the Lord's voice and not a voice that contradicts His word. *"When he has brought all his own sheep outside, he walks on ahead of them, and the sheep follow him because they know his voice and recognize his call. They will never follow a stranger, but will run away from him, because they do not know the voice of strangers."* (John 10:4–5 Amp)

When you date, who you date, and if you should date is up to the Lord and only Him. The blueprint and design for your life is not the same as the blueprint and design for your sister's life, your brother's life, or your friend's life. Your blueprint design was strategically and specifically created, formed, and molded with love, purpose, and hope, especially for you. Embrace your blueprint and every single day the Lord blesses you to wake up, wake up with gratefulness for the privilege and opportunity to fulfill your purpose and live in your hope in Him. So, as singles who date; we must date with hope, which simply means we must keep <u>Him</u> first, be <u>Observant</u>, keep His <u>Principles</u> and live with <u>Expectation</u>.

> H) <u>Him</u>: *"I have been crucified with Christ. It is no longer I who live, but Christ who lives in me. And the life I now live in the flesh I live by faith in the Son of God, who loved me and gave Himself for me."* (Galatians 2:20 NLT)

If we truly gave our life to Christ, our life died with Him on the cross. As a result, we no longer live, but it is Christ who lives on the inside of our physical shells. Our life is not about acting like Him; but it is about allowing Christ to live in us and through us. Therefore, how can we do anything without Him, including date. We do not have the right to date without the Lord's approval. As a matter of fact, we do not have the right to even accept a dinner invitation, exchange phone numbers or even chat on social media with potential individuals of interest without first praying and seeking the Lord's approval. When we do, we open ourselves up too much pain and disappointment. We must seek His guidance, acceptance, and approval. Do not continue to make the mistake of moving forward without the Lord's involvement. If we were to be honest, we have all made this mistake, so we must be willing to do things differently. I am sure we have all heard the phrase, "when you know better you do better."

Do not misunderstand what I am saying. I do not believe there is only one perfect person for each of us. Though, I do believe that there is a special person whose life can line up with our life and we can both commit and work together toward a common goal. Love is a choice of action. It is not a feeling that comes and goes. It is a decision to sacrifice for the one you chose to love, just as Christ chose to love each of us. However, we cannot love like this without Christ. This is why we must involve Him in all our decisions; and as painful and disappointing as some of His responses may be, we must accept and follow Him. He will never lead us wrong.

> o) <u>observation:</u> *Then He returned to the disciples and found them asleep. He said to Peter, "Couldn't you watch with Me even an hour? Keep watch and pray, so that you will not give in to temptation. For the spirit is willing, but the body is weak!" (Matthew 26:40–41 NIV)*

Jesus knew that in order to have victory over our struggles and over our temptations, we must always be watchful and prayerful. Jesus with His disciples had come to a place called Gethsemane, which means olive press. This is the place where olives are crushed for their oil, and it was the place where the Son of God would be crushed for our sins. The night before Jesus would be crucified on Calvary, He solicited the help of Peter and the other disciples to "watch and pray", as He went into fervent prayer about the battle He would soon have to face. Jesus knew that by watching and praying, He was directing them to use the means and the power that had been afforded unto them to use as He prepared them for life without His physical presence. Jesus knew that the disciples would fail and fall into temptation without the help and assistance of God which was readily available through the power of prayer; and my sisters and brothers, so will we.

While dating, we also must "watch and pray". There are some things that will only be revealed through the Holy Spirit. But we must be open to hearing and receiving the Lord's message. As fleshly beings, we know that emotions will be alert and active when we begin to spend time with members of the opposite sex. This is why we must stay alert (watch) to our surroundings; yet stay connected (pray) to the Lord's voice and guidance. Only God has the ability to see the heart and the intentions of the other person. So, we must be willing to receive what God reveals. Let me be clear, I am not suggesting that we are waiting on a perfect individual without weaknesses, flaws, or challenges. However, I am suggesting that God is able to weed out individuals who do not have your best interest at heart. He is able to shine the light on situations of deception that will clash with who you are designed to be.

A few years ago, a beautiful young professional woman stood and married a young man who presented himself as an entrepreneur of character and integrity. Within a few months, the truth that she refused to see and acknowledge was suddenly too much for her to bear. Shortly, thereafter (in less than a year) the pain and disappointment of a divorce followed. Months of planning and preparation went into creating the perfect wedding ceremony; while months of guidance, counsel and wisdom went ignored and rejected. The truth is, the Lord always reveals pertinent information to believers (His children). This is done to protect us. However, when God discloses this information, we must be willing to receive it. Observation is ineffective if we are not willing to receive and apply to our life the relevant information that God is allowing to be exposed for our protection.

Beloved, while dating we must be observant. We must pay attention to the person's actions. A person's words and actions must line up in order to be true. Who we are will always be exposed in how we live, the things we do, and the way we treat others? But most importantly, we must seek and maintain a close connection with the Lord, pray constantly and consistently, and ask God to give us the desire, strength, and ability to think beyond our emotions.

Again, I am not suggesting that God only has one perfect person for each of us, but I am suggesting that God can direct our paths into connection with a person who is traveling in the same direction and agree on the same doctrine. I believe this person will be willing to support, fight and sacrifice with you to accomplish similar goals and a common purpose. Additionally, this person will understand that "Holy" matrimony is a marriage ordained by God and a marriage that is precious to God; therefore, it is a marriage that should be precious to us.

P) <u>principles:</u> *"I, therefore, the prisoner of the Lord, beseech you that ye walk worthy of the vocation wherewith ye are called." (Ephesians 4:1 KJV)*

Paul writes a letter to the Christians urging them to walk worthy of their calling. As believers we should embrace this calling willingly because of God's love for us. When we really understand what God did for us, we should have an overwhelming desire to serve and obey Him out of gratefulness and gratitude. Our "worthy walk" should be humble and gentle. Yet, this walk is calling for us to meet a particular standard. It is a walk that understands that we are not in control of our life but are happy and content with walking within God's purpose. So, as we date, we must hold fast to the principles of our calling. We must recognize and embrace the fact that we have been called. Beloved, this is an invaluable position to hold. You must focus, embrace, and accept this call and the significance of the call. God chose you for a reason and a purpose. Therefore, this call is specifically designed for you and your walk.

Principles are codes of conduct. They are the fundamental laws, rules or doctrines that guide and direct our behavior. The Holy Bible was designed to set our foundation. The principles and standards laid out in the scriptures must not be compromised because of our wants and desires while dating. Trust the Holy Spirit. He can lead, guide, and keep us, but we must be willing to be kept. As believers and people of principles and purpose, we understand that we cannot continue to operate in the same manner we did prior to salvation. We are in the world but not of the world. This world is not our friend. We must be willing to do what is necessary to stay within the will of God.

When it comes to dating, there are so many "do's and don'ts". Some people suggest that Christian couples should not date without chaperones, that they should never visit each other's homes alone, that they should not kiss or show a public display of affection (such as holding hands and touching) and that they should not date for long extended periods of time. Now I do not believe we are obligated to follow everyone else's rules; however, I do believe that we must be willing to be true to ourselves and the rules of our Lord. No one knows you better than you, except for the Lord. What pushes your buttons? What ignites the internal spark of passion within you? Be honest, we must be serious about staying within the will of the Lord. The truth is our emotions are activated by physical contact. Therefore, whether you hold hands, hug or kiss while dating is something that should be determined by you and the guidance of the Holy Spirit before the possibility of a date even arises. You must know your "do's and don't's" and be willing to stand firmly on your convictions.

As dating singles, there are several areas of struggles and adjustments with which we will be faced. One very significant area of contention we will surely battle with is abstaining from sexual immorality. Although difficult, the word of God is clear.

> Run from sexual sin! No other sin so clearly affects the body as this one does. For sexual immorality is a sin against your own body. Don't you realize that your body is the temple of the Holy Spirit, who lives in you and was given to you by God? You do not belong to yourself, for God bought you with a high price. So, you must honor God with your body. (I Corinthians 6:18–20 NLT)

Unfortunately, beloved, as singles we are instructed to wait until marriage before, we can enjoy the pleasures of sexual intimacy with our husband or wife. Participating in this activity prior to marriage will lead to sexual immorality. This is considered a sin to God. Our bodies house (hold) the Holy Spirit; therefore, we are charged with maintaining a clean temple. Our temple is valuable. God paid an extremely high price for you and for me. When we truly understand

and recognize our value and worth, we will not allow cheap thrills and temporary moments of pleasure to diminish our value and defile our temple. This does not mean that we are perfect beings, but it does mean that Perfection (the Holy Spirit) lives within us. Therefore, our goal is to strive daily to walk like Christ, to remain faithful to the word and allow the Holy Spirit to do the rest.

In a previous chapter I explained that living a life of singleness is a gift from God. Therefore, if your desire is to remain single as a permanent state, you should embrace it with pride, grace, and self-confidence. God has need and purpose for you in this state. Yet, you must remember that in this state, you also choose a life of celibacy. It does not matter if you are single or married, God requires a life of holiness and righteousness. If singleness is not a permanent desire, but a chosen position by the Lord; you should still embrace it with pride, grace, and self-confidence. God loves single Christians. We are not an afterthought, overlooked or forgotten. Be assured my brothers and sisters and trust God. There is a design and plan for your life. Walk in purity, embrace your life of celibacy and watch God use you in a mighty way.

Living by the principles of Christ is not only important but essential for born-again believers. We cannot just create our own standards. The standards have already been established by the Father, the Son, and the Holy Spirit. It is now up to us to embrace them, learn them, and live by them on a daily basis. Therefore, you must ask yourself, what will you need to do to maintain the principles of the Lord? How serious are you about keeping and maintaining the principles of God? This is what will determine how you choose to live your life and what you do to protect yourself.

Now even though I do not believe we are obligated to follow everyone's rules and recommendations. I do believe that the scriptures are laid out and full of rules and principles with which we can use to establish our dating goals and standards.

E) <u>expectation:</u> *Trust in the Lord, and do good; dwell in the land, and feed on His faithfulness. Delight yourself also in the Lord, and He shall give you the desires of your heart. (Psalm 37:3–5 NKJV)*

Our expectations should always be focused on the promises of God's unconditional love for us. In Christ, we can and should expect good things to happen to and for us. As believers, we know that our ultimate goal and desire is to live in eternity with the Lord in Heaven. However, God also desires to bless us while on earth. As men and women of God, we should simply put our trust in God and strive to do good. While traveling through this journey of life we can easily get distracted, discouraged, worried and/or afraid of the trials and tribulations that knock on our door from time to time. Paul reminds believers to continue to trust God and do-good works. We must focus on enjoying the blessings that God provides as we dwell in this land. It does not matter how tough things appear to be; God is faithful.

Replace your worry and frustration with delighting yourself in the Lord. This is a deliberate and conscious action on our part to redirect our emotions to trust and rest in the Lord. We must intentionally seek solace in Jesus in times of grief, discomfort, trouble or distress. When we truly put our trust in the Lord and do good, the Lord promises to give us the desires of our heart. However, what we must realize is that when we truly begin to delight in the Lord, we will find that our heart and desires will begin to change and line up with God's will for our life. Our fleshly desires will become secondary to God's will for our life. This does not mean that God will not grant you with what you desire. This simply means that as believers, we are not to put our primary focus on fulfilling our desires but to first focus on the Lord and His will for our life.

Nevertheless, do not lose hope. We are people of hope and should live and date with hope. Hope is living with a feeling of expectation and a desire for a certain thing to happen. God desires to fulfill the heart's desire of the believer: the one who trusts Him and commits to do good works. Consequently, as you date, date with the expectation that good things will happen for you. As people of purpose, we should never date without focus, intention, and a goal. Ask yourself, why am I dating? Dating should always be with intent and with a specific goal in mind. What is your reason and goal for dating? As a Christian, you must ask yourself is it really practical for you to date without a goal in mind?

Why are you dating this person who the Holy Spirit has clearly instructed you to walk away from? Why are you dating the person who has no desire to commit? Is dating for companionship something that lines up with the principles and standards of the Word of God? It is time to ask yourself the tough questions. Come on, ask yourself, should you really be dating if you know that right now you are not in a position to commit your life in Holy Matrimony to another individual? We must be willing to sit down (refrain) until we are ready to enter into a covenant relationship. Remember, you were crucified, therefore, it is no longer you who live, but Christ who lives in you. So, whatever you do must be guided by the guidance and direction of the Holy Spirit and for the glory of God. Your purpose for dating is not about you, it is for the Glory of God. Therefore, ask yourself, does my dating life glorify the Lord?

> *"You are the salt of the earth. But what good is salt if it has lost its flavor? Can you make it salty again? It will be thrown out and trampled underfoot as worthless. "You are the light of the world—like a city on a hilltop that cannot be hidden. No one lights a lamp and then puts it under a basket. Instead, a lamp is placed on a stand, where it gives light to everyone in the house. In the same way, let your good deeds shine out for all to see, so that everyone will praise your heavenly Father."*
>
> (MATTHEW 5:13-16 NLT)

Christians are designed to influence the world in a positive way. Therefore, we must scrutinize our behavior, actions, and activities by asking ourselves, if this particular conduct and activity is going to point and lead people to Jesus. During one of the many conversations

I had with a very special and close friend, Linda Blackshear Smith, who said to me, "People do not understand the role they play in influencing other people." This is a profoundly true statement. Our actions are watched and replicated more than we realize. This is why the scriptures give specific instructions for Christians.

I Thessalonians 5:22 (KJV) instructs Christians to *"Abstain from all appearance of evil."* Appearance simply means form. We are to abstain from every form of evil. Such things as sex (penetration and/or oral), foreplay, masturbation, pornography, phone sex, and sexting are things that should not be a part of a single person's life. Again, we are not perfect beings, but we should continuously strive to be obedient to God's word. And secondly, we must always be aware and concerned with how our actions are perceived by others. Therefore, my sisters and my brothers, I lovingly ask you to ask yourself, "do the people around me see the glory of God in me and in the person in which I have committed to date"?

Never forget what a blessed people we are for the opportunity to serve God and the people of God. So, relax and enjoy your season of singleness. No one except the Lord knows exactly how long this season will last. Yet, every morning you should wake up thanking God and standing on the hope and expectation that the Lord will bless your steps, your actions, your projects, and your decisions. This time in your life can truly be a period of peace, fulfilment, and gratification. God desires to use your life for His glory. But you must be willing to trust Him, listen for His soft still voice and quickly move to follow His instructions. We are blessed people. We are people of love and people of hope. So, my single sisters and brothers, continue to commit your lives to the Lord with joy, with trust and with patience. The Lord has not forgotten about you. Never doubt how much He loves you. We must trust Him and His plan for our life. He truly does understand your longing for love and companionship. He can also see that deep-rooted internal desire to marry. Therefore, we must know without a shadow of a doubt that *".… the LORD will withhold no good thing from those who do what is right."* (Psalm 84:11 NLT) Thus, Beloved, you must trust and believe that one day God will have that special someone waiting for you at the end of the aisle.

6

Eternal Commitment

"Be ye not unequally yoked together with unbelievers: for what fellowship has righteousness with unrighteousness? and what communion hath light with darkness? And what concord hath Christ with Belial? or what part hath he that believeth with an infidel? And what agreement hath the temple of God with idols? for ye are the temple of the living God; as God hath said, I will dwell in them, and walk in them; and I will be their God, and they shall be my people."
—II CORINTHIANS 6:14–16 (KJV)

Yes!!! He finally popped the question: will you marry me? Now the engagement begins. What does this actually mean? What is engagement? The dictionary definition explains engagement as a betrothal or espousal. It states that this is a mutual agreement, promise or contract for a future marriage. After speaking with a few individuals, I would like to share some of their personal definitions of engagement.

Engagement is:

- A couple who is committed but has not reached the official sealing of the commitment that comes with marriage.

Everything changes, you are committed to a particular person but at this point you are not subject to receive all the benefits that come along with marriage, i.e., living together, sex, intimacy; however, you are preparing for that moment.

- Two people coming together with plans for a future marriage.
- More than a relationship. We as a couple have moved to the next step towards marriage. It is like climbing a ladder, step by step.
- The couple has decided to enter into a monogamous relationship. They have decided to set themselves apart with the goal of entering into a marriage.
- That the couple's intentions are to get married, which is the next step. Engagement means that there is no intimacy (sexual) until marriage, but this couple is preparing for marriage. They are committed to each other, only spending time with each other and only thinking about each other.

I believe we all understand that engagement is the period between dating and marriage. I also believe we understand and accept that engagement is a mutual agreement or a promise between a man and woman to enter into a future marriage. But let us be realistic. Do we all understand the significance of that commitment? What does it mean to make a commitment? The dictionary describes commitment as the act of committing, pledging, or engaging oneself. Which means when you make a commitment you are making a pledge, a promise, or an obligation to do something. I am sure we can all agree that the biblical definition/meaning of engagement is not the exact principle that we follow in today's society. For example, when a couple breaks or calls off an engagement, it is not considered a divorce, which was necessary in biblical days. However, as believers, we are still supposed to embrace the principle and meaning of commitment. We must understand the significance and importance of keeping our words, promises and commitments. The truth is, by the time the mutual agreement is made to enter into marriage there should be absolutely no reservations within your spirit. You should be completely at peace that God will cover and keep your marriage and that He (the Lord) is ordering your steps.

Please do not misunderstand me, I get the reservations and reluctance of the possibility of having to suffer through the pain of marrying the wrong person. Therefore, as a result many choose to date for many years and/or even share living quarters instead of embracing the courage to make that commitment. However, there is an opposite reaction where some couples rush into marrying the wrong person because they date for a short period of time and they are literally floating in clouds of emotions and excitement. How do we know when it is the right time and the right person to actually make the commitment to marry? Trust me, I understand. I wish I could give you an absolute guaranteed answer, but I cannot. However, I can tell you about an absolute necessary tool that is available only to born again believers for your decision-making process. This tool is simply the gift of the Holy Spirit. The indwelling of Jesus Christ within the body of the believer is the "essential" wisdom and guidance that we often fail to lean on, trust, follow and obey.

While we as a nation battle with the COVID 19 pandemic in the year of 2020, we often hear the television news reporters speak about essential workers. For them, this country is eternally grateful. However, as believers, we have personal access to another essential worker. I can with confidence assure you that the number one Essential Worker that we should seek in our everyday lives while making everyday decisions is the Holy Spirit. The Holy Spirit indwells in the heart and spirit of believers as a guide and counselor. Jesus Christ left believers the comfort of the Holy Spirit for our protection. Yet, we often choose to ignore His voice and direction. The Lord knows which person is designed for our life. However, He will not force us to follow His voice. We must be willing to yield to His voice and then listen and obey His instructions in order to avoid the pain, dangers, and relationship disasters that many of us have suffered in the past.

As believers, we cannot just float around in an emotional cloud. Our heart is precious to the Lord; therefore, it is extremely important to whom we choose to release it. (Proverbs 4:20-23 NLT with emphasis on verse 23) "My child, pay attention to what I say. Listen carefully to my words. Don't lose sight of them. Let them penetrate deep into your heart, for they bring life to those who find them, and healing to their whole body. *Guard your heart above all else, for it determines the course of your life."* We are instructed to guard our hearts which basically means to be alert and place a watchman over our hearts. This would require us to stream our emotions, desires, thoughts, feelings, and choices through Jesus and through His Word. When we stay focused on God's word and committed to the principles of the Lord, He (the Lord) will keep our hearts. Proverbs 4:23 emphasizes that the human heart is the very core of a person's being. It is where our thoughts, emotions and desires are generated, spoken, and acted upon. Therefore, Proverbs Chapter 4 teaches that as believers we must seek and live in Godly wisdom by following the instructions and corrections of God's wisdom. This is where we gain direction and protection over our lives.

As we stay committed to focusing on Jesus and His word, I believe there are certain things that should stand firm in importance as we choose our life partner. Yes, that's right, this is a decision that was designed by the Word of God to last. This commitment was meant to not be broken; therefore, it is not to be taken lightly. This is why we cannot trust our feelings and emotions, nor are we to rely on them. The Holy Spirit is our golden ticket in this process. So, the most important aspect of this process is knowing without a shadow of a doubt that you have both committed your lives to Jesus Christ. "Be ye not unequally yoked together with unbelievers: for what fellowship hath righteousness with unrighteousness? ..." (II Corinthians 6:14 KJV)

The scriptures teach "and the two shall become one flesh ..." (Mark 10:8 NKJV). This type of intimacy can only be created when you are joined together in Christ, because at that point the two of you share the same spirit and the same source of love. Without this spiritual bond you risk living within a divided marital union. God instructs in scripture that believers are not to partner with unbelievers, for what fellowship (partnership) can righteousness have with unrighteousness (lawlessness). It does not matter that they may be handsome, beautiful, fine, sexy, financially secure, or may even have a nice personality. Brethren, God's instructions are clear. To marry an unbeliever would mean that you are first acting in disobedience to God's word which always comes with a consequence. Secondly, you risk being influenced by principles and standards that do not line up with the word of God. Yet, the blessing of marrying another believer is that by doing things God's way, the Holy Spirit who lives within you is the same Holy Spirit who lives within your mate.

Human beings are incapable of loving on the level and magnitude that the Lord will urge and direct. We are selfish by nature, but the power of the Holy Spirit will lead and place desires within your heart on how to love your spouse. There will be things that you do not like doing nor want to do; but will be motivated and compelled to do in order to help, encourage and love your mate. This will be the result of the direction and wisdom of the Holy Spirit. Will your marriage be without trials, tribulations, and heartache? Absolutely not, but the covering, guidance, direction, and peace of the Holy Spirit is a gift that is only accessible to believers. Trust me, you do not want to endure an earthly marriage without it. Godly marriages are blessings from heaven; yet, they do not come without problems and issues. However, with the help of the Holy Spirit and your free will submission to His counsel, there is no problem that you and your spouse will not be able to overcome together.

Another important aspect to consider before deciding to move into a committed engagement is communication. Healthy communication is critical for successful relationships. Are the two of you able to have open and honest conversations. Can you trust this person with your inner most thoughts, concerns and issues? Listen, my brothers and sisters, I do not care how sweet you believe your mate to be, conflict and disagreements are unavoidable. It is important that the two of you are able to resolve conflict in a healthy, reasonable and Godly manner.

Several years ago, a male cousin, seriously advised me to never enter a committed relationship with a man until I have seen how he acts when he gets angry. My cousin literally said to me, "even if you have to intentionally do something to make him mad, you need to know how he responds when he is angry." Now at the time I thought that was really strange advice, plus I do not have the personality to intentionally provoke someone to anger. However, I learned that the truth is, you do not have to intentionally provoke someone ... conflict and disagreements are unavoidable; believe me, it will happen. So,

EVANGELINE RENTZ

when they do, take the advice of my cousin, and pay close attention to how your partner responds.

Many years ago, I attracted the attention of a certain young man. For several years I received numerous attempts of contact, such as phone calls and emails, expressing in great detail his interest and attraction. Honestly, his attraction flattered me. However, there was always some reason that the connection and physical meeting never actually took place. Time would pass, months and sometimes years, and suddenly, he would resurface and continue in his pursuit. Well, conflict and disagreement soon surfaced and this young man's angry response to a particular situation confirmed for me that at that particular time, I could not be comfortable trusting him with my heart.

Now please do not misunderstand me, no argument feels good. Therefore, when you enter into a committed relationship please understand that neither party is perfect in that relationship. Sin is forever present, and sin actively works to influence our behaviors by activating our selfish, insensitive, and hostile reactions. No one is exempt from this. We have all been influenced by sin and responded inappropriately through our behavior. Therefore, as believers we should recognize that we do not " ...wrestle against flesh and blood, but against principalities, against powers, against the rulers of the darkness of this age, against spiritual hosts of wickedness in the heavenly places." (Ephesians 6:12 NKJV) Meaning we must be willing to separate the sin from the individual (our partner). We must understand that if we both succumb and respond to our selfish urges; a simple disagreement can grow, escalate, and explode like a volcano that is impossible to control and contain.

Thus, as for my former pursuer, I choose to trust and believe that the power of the Holy Spirit who resides within him will prevail. I pray that his future relationship will be blessed and that he embraces conflict and disagreement by choosing to fight against sinful and selfish urges to carelessly respond. I pray that he expresses his responses in love by choosing to react with the heart and character of Christ. Remember, conflict and disagreement are unavoidable yet necessary. The individuals within the relationship must have the liberty and freedom to disagree without the fear of being verbally attacked. When appropriately handled, disagreements can promote healthy relationships because the individuals are allowed to be sincere and honest. Therefore, if you cannot be open and honest, you should seriously consider if you should move forward with the relationship; if you are not able to truly be the person that God created you to be. Think about that. Is this how you want to live the rest of your life, by suppressing the real you? Consequently, before you commit make sure you have the peace of God within, that you both are able to openly be yourselves and that you are able to resolve conflicts or disagreements through the wisdom and love of Christ.

Keep in mind, there are many other things that should be considered before agreeing to enter into a committed engagement. However, you should seek your guidance and counsel from the Holy Spirit and the Word of God. This is a serious step, and we must be diligent in our pursuit of truth. This life is not about our feelings and desires. It is so much larger than that. Remember, as we previously discussed, everything we do should be to the glory of God. Our agreements and commitment to an earthly engagement should be just as serious as our commitment to a life with Christ. Bad relationships and toxic marriages do not bring glory to God. So, trust His guidance and seek His voice with diligence and determination. As believers, it should be our heart's desire to be true to our word. Therefore, before you commit and pledge your heart to another individual, examine your relationship closely. Be honest and true to what you see, what you learn, and to the voice of Christ. Beloved, you do not have to fight for someone to love you. Jesus loves you, and He chooses to indwell within you waiting to connect you through His Spirit to the person that He has designed for your life. Trust His plan, trust His love, and wait patiently for His approval to eternally commit until death do you two part.

7

Naked and Not Ashamed

Therefore a man shall leave his father and mother and be joined to his wife, and they shall become one flesh. And they were both naked, the man and his wife, and were not ashamed.

—Genesis 2:24–25 (NKJV)

As I sit to pen this particular chapter, I am reminded of a moment in time several years ago when an attractive young man named Evan heavily began his pursuit to win the attention of a beautiful young woman named Christine. Evan was extremely attractive, I mean FINE!! He was educated, professional, and appeared to be financially secure. He was tall, slim, sexy and to put the icing on the cake, this man professed Christianity. Now, I know you are saying, what more can a woman ask for. Well hold on, there is so much more to this story. Evan expressed to Christine numerous times over the years how attracted he was to her. He told her that he thought she was beautiful, sexy, and sweet. He said that he loved her character traits and the fact that she had a relationship with Christ. Evan's attention and compliments really delighted Christine.

Well time passed and Evan was ready to finally meet Christine. So, he sent her an email, yes, an email. The email informed Christine that he was going to be in the area where she lived on a particular weekend, and that he would like for them to finally meet. However, the email he sent began by stating, "I am aware that you are planning on being out of town on that weekend…". As a result, Christine responded by stating, "I would love to meet you, however, as you are aware, I will not be in town on the weekend that you are scheduled to be in town." After Christine's response, things went south. Evan immediately responded back and told Christine that she had two weeks to change her plans. Therefore, Christine decided to stop responding, but Evan kept writing. In his several responses that followed, he asked Christine if she had changed her plans and why she was not responding. He told her that she was acting immature by failing to respond. He declared that as a Christian she was supposed to be loving. He asked her how she can be loving when she was acting so "unconcerned and wicked". Evan finally exclaimed in an email to Christine, "who are you to reject me!"

Two weeks passed and Christine kept her travel plans and had a fantastic time, but when she returned from her trip … oh my!! Christine received a long email from Evan stating he wanted to come clean. In the email he told her that he never wanted anything but a friendship with her. He stated he was not physically attracted to her because of her size and that her skin complexion was too dark for him. He told her that he was aware that she was attracted to men that looks like him but that she was going to have to lower her standards, because a man who looks like him would never be caught with a woman who looks like her.

Christine was very reluctant about opening her closet and being totally transparent regarding this personal situation. However, she soon surrendered to the guidance of the Holy Spirit and agreed that if what she went through will help someone else, she was willing to share her story and her pain. Because truthfully, Evan's response CRUSHED her. Christine kept replaying his words from the email over and over and over again in her head until she finally broke. One day, she hit the floor in her bedroom and just cried her eyes out. Moments later she pulled herself together, but she completely lost it again while she was visiting with a close friend. She could not understand what she did to deserve such treatment. She never would have done anything to intentional hurt him. She just did not understand. She did not pursue him, she did not call him, she did not initiate emails or contact with him. He sought after her contact information and He contacted her, numerous times. So, Christine did not and could not understand why he would believe that she deserved such an intentional act of verbal mistreatment and abuse. And although she wrestled internally with these thoughts, the truth is because Christine was a strong woman of faith, it only lasted for a moment. Thank You Lord!!!!!

You see, in the midst of that pain, in the midst of that hurt, the Holy Spirit spoke and reminded Christine that He loved her, and that she was beautiful; not just internally, but externally. The Holy Spirit comforted her spirit to help her understand that the Lord allowed this painful situation so that she could see the current condition of the heart of the man that she thought she desired to be with. God assured Christine in her moment of hurt, disappointment, and discouragement that if she continues to trust Him, He promises to keep her and that He would withhold no good thing from her. As the Lord comforted Christine, He reaffirmed to her heart that the man He designed specifically for her … will see her the way that He sees her, he will respect her the way that He respects her, and he will protect her the way that He protects her.

The Holy Spirit clearly spoke into Christine's spirit that day to remind her to never minimize or allow anyone else to make her question, or second guess her beauty or her value in who He has created her to be. God desires that she never forget that she is His design and that there is no one who is able to design a greater more precious creation!!! Wow, I must confess, that that special moment in time that Christine shared with the Lord truly deserved an Amen!!!

First, let me start by saying Christine has confessed to completely forgiving Evan. Seriously, she has absolutely no anger or contention in her heart regarding him. She is prayerful that over the years Evan has allowed the Lord to heal the pain and hurt that dwells deep within him. And she really believes that one day he will walk in the call that God created and destined specifically for him. You see, even though this experience was painful for Christine, it became clear to her that this young man's verbal response was birthed and rooted in pain, his pain. Think about it, I am sure you have heard the quote, "hurt people, hurt people." It's true, but the problem is that we oftentimes refuse to acknowledge our pain and our brokenness. As a result, we choose not to seek assistance to work towards healing and restoration. Consequently, we leave behind a trail of lives along this journey who have been hurt, broken, and maybe even destroyed due to our hands and actions.

But there is hope. God has a way of touching the broken and restoring our lives for His glory. God can get the glory out of our lives, out of our mistakes, and out of our pain. If we choose to submit and trust Him. I share the story of Evan and Christine, not only for the ones who are experiencing hurt, disappointment, and verbal mistreatment, but also for the ones who are executing the hurt by their words, hands, and actions. Beloved, God can heal your pain, if you choose to let Him. The Lord loves you and He is waiting and willing for you to allow Him to heal your brokenness and redirect your path towards a journey of peace and true love.

There is nothing more beautiful than a romantic and loving relationship between a man and a woman, a husband, and his wife. We dream about it, we fantasize about it, we desire it, and we stop at nothing to attain it. But at what cost? The young man that pursued Christine for months, professed to care deeply for her, yet, in a moment of anger, he intentionally, set out to hurt her. What is it that happens in that moment that erases all feelings, all of the consideration, and all of the respect for the person you "say" you love and care about? Come on, how can you care for someone one day and become completely unconcerned about how you treat them and speak to them the next day?

Well, I am no longer only talking about Evan. I am talking to everyone reading this book. Because truthfully, most of us have all been there. In a moment of rage, anger, or disappointment we speak words that pierce the very soul of our love ones that we can never take back. In this book we have taken a journey together. A journey that deals with love and relationships under God's design. We have discussed God's creation and the ultimate plan of the return of the Bridegroom. We have talked about embracing our purpose, maximizing the moment of our current state, dating, and engagement. So now it is time to talk about marriage, holy matrimony.

In Genesis, Chapter 2, the Lord indicates a man is joined together with his wife and the two of them become <u>one flesh</u>. The scripture goes on to state that they were both naked, and not ashamed. Think about that for a moment … a husband and his wife, were naked and not ashamed. I believe God was speaking of much more than the fact that Adam and Eve were without clothing. When you think about the Garden of Eden, when you think about that place, you cannot help but visualize a beautiful, serene, and peaceful paradise. A place of pure beauty where everything was perfect. The love was perfect, the romance was perfect, the communication was perfect, the trust was perfect, because at that time (pre-sin) their relationship with God was pure, constant, important, intimate, and perfect.

Naked represents a certain degree of vulnerability, trust, transparency, and realness. Can I be transparent, open, and real with you? Can I be comfortable showing you my flaws, my weaknesses, my scars, and insecurities? Can I reveal myself completely to you and you love me totally and unconditionally, in the midst of my flaws? Can I trust you with my inner-most thoughts, desires, goals, and dreams? Can I trust you to love me when I make mistakes and disappoint you? Can I trust you to protect me physically, spiritually, and emotionally? Can I trust you with my heart? <u>Can I truly be Naked and Not Ashamed</u> in your presence?

These are deep and serious questions for us to consider. God created man and woman and placed them together in the Garden of Eden as husband and wife and they were naked and not ashamed. God created and ordained marriage to glorify Him. It is a spiritual covenant that is meant to be an earthly example of Christ's relationship with the church. Our marriage should bring God glory. When there is no trust, no transparency or vulnerability … when you are miserable, not communicating, or engaging in verbal or physical abuse, how does that marriage glorify God?

In this particular set of scriptures, naked and nude may not necessarily mean the same thing. Nude is defined as completely unclothed or undressed. Unfortunately, we may not want to admit this, but many people have gone out for a night on the town, met someone and took our clothes off that very same evening or shortly thereafter. Even though you were nude, you did not know the person, therefore you were incapable of being totally transparent or vulnerable. Nude only shows a person our physical body, the outside shell. Yet being naked reveals to a person your physical body as well as your emotional and mental well-being. It is a sense of being totally open and exposed as a person before the Lord and before your mate. When we are with our spouses, there should be nothing to be ashamed of and nothing to hide.

When we are in right relationship with the Lord, we can be totally comfortable being open and vulnerable with absolutely nothing to hide. The scripture states the "two shall become one flesh ……" (Mark 10:8 NKJV) There is no place for secrecy in a God-ordained marriage. Do not misunderstand me. There will be times when alone time and privacy is necessary, such as, moments of prayer, meditation or shared counsel between you and another individual. However, privacy is not secrecy. Secrecy means the condition of being hidden or concealed which implies that there is something about you or something going on with you that you cannot trust your mate with. When you are a husband or a wife this is a problem. Being vulnerable opens you up to being hurt, so many try to avoid this by putting a fence/wall around our heart to keep from being hurt. As a result, we will never be able to experience the true nature of a covenant relationship without nakedness, exposure, and vulnerability.

The question becomes are you in a committed pre-marital relationship (dating or engaged) with an individual with whom you cannot be open, honest, and vulnerable? Are you contemplating dating or permanently connecting with a person with whom you are unable to be naked and not ashamed? Are you willing to give up the opportunity to experience love the way God designed for love to be?

This type of relationship is not without intentionality. It is the state of being deliberate or purposeful. This type of relationship is not created automatically, it takes work and effort. The individuals involved in this covenant relationship are intentional about the care and concern delivered by them to their mate. Their words are intentional, their actions are intentional, and their motives are intentional. Not intentional to hurt, abuse, or mistreat; but, intentional to provide love, protection, care, and respect, even when the two of you disagree. Your flaws, weaknesses, and insecurities are safe and always protected by this person to whom you committed your life, the *one to whom you chose to become one.*

A relationship where a husband and wife can totally be naked and not ashamed, is the relationship designed by God and covered in unconditional love. It is a relationship that is guided by the principles of Christ and covered by the love of Christ. So, let's talk about some practical ways for us to consider that will help us create passionate and fulfilling covenant relationships where we can truly be <u>Naked and Not Ashamed</u>.

1. <u>Keep Christ first in your marriage:</u> "Either way, Christ's love controls us. Since we believe that Christ died for all, we also believe that we have all died to our old life. He died for everyone so that those who receive his new life will no longer live for themselves. Instead, they will live for Christ, who died and was raised for them." (II Corinthians 5:14–15 NLT)

Before sin, Adam and Eve were able to commune with God in a peaceful and serene place. That covenant was broken the moment sin took root. But when Christ died on the cross for our sins, that changed. As a result, His love should compel and motivate us to love and serve as He does. When we keep Christ in the center of our marriage, we focus on loving, reacting, and responding as He would. According to the teaching of the scripture, when we gave our life to Christ our old life died, and we received a new life in Him. Therefore, we no longer live for ourselves, but for Christ. The very nature of a Christian is to live for Christ. Therefore, everything in your life should be built on the foundation and principles of Christ, including our marriage.

2. <u>Deal with conflict and confrontation Biblically:</u> "Be angry, and do not sin": do not let the sun go down on your wrath," (Ephesians 4:26 NKJV)

Remember, conflict and disagreements are inevitable. Therefore, how we respond will determine the healthiness of our relationship. Poor communication is one of the leading problems in marriages and is still a critical reason marriage ends in divorce. Thus, we must be willing to work on our communication skills.

The reality is in marriage we will sin against one another from time to time because as humans we have not reached perfection. As a result, there will be times when you will be selfish, inconsiderate, irritable, and not easy to get along with. During those moments, " … do not let the sun go down while you are still angry." (Ephesians 4:26 NIV) Sit down and be willing to talk about it. There is "no issue" that cannot be resolved through Christ and good communication.

3. <u>Develop and enjoy a healthy sex-life with your spouse:</u> Now for the matters you wrote about: "It is good for man not to have sexual relations with a woman." But since sexual immorality is occurring, each man should have sexual relations with his own wife, and each woman with her own husband. The husband should fulfill his marital duty to his wife, and likewise the wife to her husband. The wife does not have authority over her own body but yields it to her husband. In the same way, the husband does not have authority over his own body but yields it to his wife. Do not deprive each other except perhaps by mutual consent and for a time, so that you may devote yourselves to prayer. Then come together again so that Satan will not tempt you because of your lack of self-control. (I Corinthians 7:1–5 NIV)

Our body is not our own. Paul teaches that we have a divine duty in marriage to one another sexually. It is not right to withhold affection from your spouse. Now, please do not misunderstand. As Godly husbands and wives our number one goal is to be considerate of what our mate is going through at the moment. Just because he or she is not in the mood to sexually perform at the moment does not mean they are withholding. There could be many sensible reasons for the refusal. The key principle here is that sex should never be used as punishment. This not only keeps you pure from temptation, but it builds your intimacy with one another.

4. Develop and maintain genuine emotional and intellectual intimacy: "Therefore shall a man leave his father and his mother and shall cleave unto his wife: and they shall be one flesh." (Genesis 2:24 KJV)

In most cases there is no earthly relationship that is closer to a person than their mother and father. There is no greater bond on earth than that of a child and the parents that came together to bring them into existence. Yet God tells us that not even that relationship is to come before the relationship between a husband and his wife. Being "one flesh" is to develop true, emotional, and intellectual intimacy with your spouse. Your spouse should be your best friend, your number one cheerleader, and the one person you can count on. This is why you should be open, honest and completely "naked" with this person. You should always speak the truth in love. This is the way you develop trust and transparency. This is God's design and process whereby the two become one flesh.

5. Lastly, always be thankful for the spouse God gave you. "Let your wife be a fountain of blessing for you. Rejoice in the wife of your youth. She is a loving deer, a graceful doe. Let her breasts satisfy you always. May you always be captivated by her love." (Proverbs 5:18–19 NLT)

Do not let the world, the media, social media, and television give you an unrealistic view or expectation of marriage. Learn to be satisfied and content with the spouse God has given you. With intention learn and work on how to be committed and content with the person you married. Work daily on fulfilling your covenant obligations to that person and only with that individual. Rejoice and appreciate them fully (physically, emotionally, and sexually) including flaws and imperfections. And do not forget to enjoy sexual intimacy often, and do not worry, God approves.

Beloved, naked, and not ashamed, is a covenant "marital" relationship that is created through God's guidance and your obedience. Like Adam and Eve in the Garden of Eden before sin interrupted their lives; it was a relationship of peace and serenity. In this relationship a couple is completely comfortable being totally open and honest with each other as they spend their lives together, communing with God.

8

The Invitation

"Nothing evil will be allowed to enter, nor anyone who practices shameful idolatry and dishonesty-but only those whose names are written in the Lamb's Book of Life."
—Revelation 21:27 (NLT)

At last, the day has come. You have prayed, you have prepared, you have followed the voice of God and now the day is finally here. We have taken the journey through this book together and we have embraced our God given purpose. Our love for Christ has transformed our lives to live for Him. We made an eternal commitment to live in the likeness of Christ and to walk in "Holiness and Righteousness". We have embraced our life's journey with patience, satisfaction, and integrity. But most importantly, we willingly and humbly serve the Kingdom of God and the people of God with zeal, excitement and vigor while awaiting the moment to celebrate the covenant of our unification with our One true love.

I believe most "earthly" wives will agree that it is the most amazing feeling to wake up on their wedding day. The day when you get dressed and prepare to walk down the aisle to meet the man of your dreams and become his bride. It is one of the greatest and most fulfilling moments in a person's life. That moment when you vow to connect to a person for eternity on your wedding day.

I absolutely love receiving wedding invitations. To receive such an invitation means I have been chosen to attend one of the most intimate, exquisite, and special events of a person's life. It is an invitation that is specifically designed for a chosen group of people. What an honor! Do you really think about what a blessing it is for someone to select you to attend one of the most significant events of their life? The moment when the couple stands before God to commit spiritually, publicly, and verbally to spend the rest of their lives with that one particular individual. It is an incredible moment that is recorded in heaven and sketched in the hearts of the wedding guests forever. What a magnificent opportunity to have been chosen to not only witness this glorious affair but to have been included as a part of the celebration.

As God poured this book within my spirit to share with you, I was led to reflect on weddings and all the wedding invitations I have received over the years. I am truly saddened by the fact that I did not recognize the magnitude of such a privilege and honor to have been chosen to receive such an invitation. When I think about how significant it was for my name to have been chosen to be placed on someone's wedding guest list, I am now enlightened to the overwhelming privilege of such an honor. Think about it. This invitation has been specifically granted to a select group of people. As I think about weddings, I do not know of one single situation where the bride and groom opened the door so that "any and every" individual within the community would have the opportunity to come in and be a part of their special wedding celebration. The "engaged" couple always come together to communicate and make a decision on whose names will be added to the elite list of individuals who will receive an invitation to attend this glorious affair and share this incredible moment with the bride and groom.

While writing this book, I am reminded of a very powerful and touching testimony of a young professional singer. This particular young woman was invited to sing at one of the most prestigious wedding celebrations in the community. Her experience and testimony regarding this invitation touched my heart in such a profound way.

Like many of us, she received the wedding invitation and the enclosed card to RSVP her acceptance as a guest to the reception celebration. The abbreviation RSVP stands for répondez s'il vous plait, and it simply means to please reply. Therefore, the event host is expecting the invitees to reply to the invitation by indicating whether they plan to attend. Yet, the soloist became too busy to respond to the RSVP, assuming that because of her role in the wedding ceremony (or like many of us our relationship with the wedding couple) that she and her guest will be automatically granted an entrance to attend the exclusive reception. The event was expected to be a grand affair with the community's most elite and wealthiest families in attendance. The wedding soloist was extremely excited about being a chosen part of such an elaborate celebration. Yet, she failed to properly prepare for the moment. She failed to follow the rules and instructions that were required for all reception participates. As a result, when the grand moment arrived, she missed the opportunity to be a part of the celebration. After the wedding she stood with her husband to enter the reception hall as the maître d checked the guest list. Her name was not included on the guest list for the wedding reception; therefore, she was not permitted entrance into this spectacular event.

According to statistical data found on the internet, approximately sixty-two million couples got married in the United States in 2019. Now I cannot confirm that the internets' data is completely accurate. However, the point I am trying to make is that based on that number, it is obvious that a tremendous amount of wedding invitations went out that year. People are still constantly receiving invitations to attend weddings. We check our calendars and make a decision on whether to accept or deny the invitation based on the couple getting married, our availability, the location of venue, and the popularity of the guests on the list. Although this may or may not be appropriate for "earthly" wedding invitations, there is one invitation that stands above all others.

It is the most vital invitation you will ever receive. It is an invitation that is sent by the Lord Himself to attend the most glorious wedding ceremony that will ever take place. Beloved, the invitations have already been sent; yet, sadly many people have failed to <u>accept</u> and <u>respond</u> to the Lord's invitation. In Romans 10:9 (NKJV) the scripture teaches that *"if you confess with your mouth the Lord Jesus and believe in your heart that God has raised Him from the dead, you will be saved* [emphasis added]." Beloved, the conditional term "if" indicates that there is something that you must do in order to receive salvation. You must be willing to accept the Lord's condition by confessing and believing. According to the Holy Bible, salvation only comes when we choose to accept His invitation. Without your acceptance you will not be permitted to attend the ultimate wedding celebration and your name will not appear in the Lamb's Book of Life. Once we accept the Lord's invitation the scriptures and the Holy Spirit begin to teach us about our walk with the Lord and our commitment to Christ. As followers of Christ, we now become the sheep of Christ. And God's word states, "My sheep hear My voice, and I know them, and they follow Me." (John 10:27 NKJV).

The Lord has chosen the church as His bride. Yet, the sad truth is that every individual sitting on the pews in the "brick and mortar church" building does not represent the church. *"For many are called, but few are chosen." (Matthew 22:14 NKJV)* Your activities in the church, such as singing in the choir, serving on the trustee board, teaching Bible study, or preaching in the pulpit does not automatically place your name on the guest list. Your church work does not automatically make you eligible to attend the ultimate wedding reception celebration. The true church is represented by the individual(s) who willingly accepts the Lord's call and responds to His invitation. You must RSVP. Have you accepted His invitation? Have you made yourself ready for His return? Is your name written in the Lamb's Book of Life and on Heaven's guest list? Where is His Bride? Where is the one who has made herself ready?

Where is she? She is currently walking the earth representing the One she loves. She serves the kingdom, she nurtures the broken, she embraces the brokenhearted, she supports the lonely, she feeds the hungry, she clothes the naked, she educates the lost and she loves all of humankind. Yes, the Lord's Bride is presently intentional about the choices she makes. She is purposeful and deliberate with her actions, in the places she travels and in the people with whom she chooses to socialize. The Lord's Bride is determined and calculated about her overall lifestyle. She is faithful, she is trustworthy, she is committed, and she is firm on her convictions from the Word of God because she has been chosen and set aside to become One with the Word.

She is not perfect; yet she is loyal to Him and only Him. "My sheep hear My voice, and I know them, and they follow Me." (John 10:27 NKJV) Consequently, her desires and her attention are solely focused on pleasing Him. My sisters and brothers, faithfulness is a critical component to any committed relationship. No one desires an unfaithful spouse, including the Lord. Remember, He is looking for the one dressed in "clean and white" attire. Commitment is not an option. It is a calculated and chosen attribute that is necessary in all loving relationships and most importantly in our walk with Christ.

Jesus will one day return to receive His bride. The one who has made herself ready. The one who follows His lead and lives according to His Word and His example. The one that is clothed in holiness and righteousness. The one who is actively preparing for that great wedding day. She presently walks the earth in oneness with her Savior and Lord as she serves His earthly kingdom as His loving ambassador. She willingly denies her flesh and allows the Lord to use her as a vessel to teach His word, make disciples, and appeal the lost into submission, repentance, and salvation. Her heart is filled with excitement as she eagerly awaits the moment when she stands face to face with her Bridegroom to consummate the vow she already made in her heart. The tears flow, her knees buckle and her heart flutters as she anticipates the moment when she looks upon His face. His glory covers her as the Divine unification is now complete. *"And the city has no need of sun or moon, for the glory of God illuminates the city, and the Lamb is its light." (Revelation 21:23 NLT)*

Where is the Lord's Bride? Where is this incredible being that is committed to becoming one with Him? She looks like Him, she dresses like Him, she serves like Him and she loves like Him. She is rare, unique, dedicated, and humble. But most importantly, she is chosen, set aside, and consecrated by Him as she patiently awaits her special day. The wedding is indeed an incredible event that is meant to be both special and exquisite. It is a moment that should be entered into following dedicated prayer and intentional planning and preparation. It is a moment where man and woman have made the decision to commit in total submission to each other through the trials and tribulations of life, through the sickness and health, and through the rich and the poor. It is a covenant union where love is professed, embraced, and vowed to last forever.

That day, the great wedding day (whether earthly or spiritual), is specifically designed and prepared only for the ones who have made themselves ready. Therefore, we must understand that we cannot live and do what we want and be saved. Salvation is about repentance, repentance is about change, and change is about transformation. We are designed to be new creatures [creations]; old things have passed away. You are not the same. My brothers and sisters, I lovingly plead with you to not forsake the Lord's invitation. Accept, embrace, and cherish His invitation with pride and dedication. Listen for His voice, follow His directions and focus on your purpose and preparation.

As you delight yourself in the Lord, the Lord wishes to fulfil the desires of your heart. But you must focus on His design for marriage and trust His plan for your life. Fret not yourself, my brothers and sisters, God will bless and grant many of us an answer to our prayers for an earthly marriage. However, we must be prepared. Marriage is not easy. Marriages like the thorny rose bush can be both "exquisite and excruciating". Therefore, we must learn how to nurture and handle marriages with care and attention in order to bring out the very essence of its beauty. So, we must remain committed to the Lord's principles and standards. Do not betray your First Love. Are you really the Lord's Bride?

Born again believers were created and designed to one day become beautiful brides. One day the preparation, the sacrifice, the sleepless nights, the long hours of work and service will all be worth it as we stand at the altar to unite with our husband (earthly and/or spiritual). However, this particular "earthly" bride is special and rare, because this bride is also the committed "spiritual" bride of Christ. She is beautiful, her character is holy, her gown is splendid, and her presence illuminates the light and glory of Christ. The sanctuary is decorated to perfection and the peace and solace that fills the room are breathtaking. What a moment!! No other moment will ever compare to the beauty and splendor of this wedding celebration.

My brothers and my sisters, are you ready? Are you currently committed to preparing for the Lord's return? If for some chance you are not, please stop and make a commitment right now to start. It is not too late to accept the Lord's invitation, but one day it will be. Therefore, choose to say yes, right now, because tomorrow is not promised. And then, at that point when you hear the Lord whisper in your spirit, where is My bride; you will be able to confidently look in the mirror at your beautiful reflection and proudly confess and proclaim," Here I am Lord, here I am!!"

Expressions from the Heart

Personal Journal

_____

_____

_____

_____

_____

_____

_____

_____

_____

_____

_____

About the Author

Evangelist Evangeline "Angie" Rentz was born and raised in Palmetto, FL. She is the fourth child of six children, and one God-sister, to Harry and Annie Mae Rentz. Evangeline is a graduate of Florida State University where she received a Bachelor of Science degree in Consumer Economics with a minor in Business.

In the year 2001, God began to minister to her about her life as a chosen woman of God. After the period of preparation, in the year 2004, her assignment was given. God instructed her to provide an outlet to allow individuals to come, vent, learn, receive encouragement, instructions, and sometimes deliverance from one of the toughest areas that we deal with … (love and relationships).

This assignment started her "Love Fellowship Luncheon" sessions, where men and women (solo and combined) would gather, fellowship, laugh, cry, talk, and learn about "love and relationships under God's design." As a result of this ministry, Evangelist Rentz has hosted several conferences, conducted many workshops, and accepted numerous preaching and speaking engagements to preach and teach on this awesome subject.

Evangeline is committed to working for the Lord and the Kingdom of God. In addition to writing and working within her God given assignment, she has previously and graciously labored for many years within the Church Music Ministry Department, served as the Women of Wisdom (WOW) Women's Ministry President, and the Church School Adult and Bible Study Instructor. Evangeline is currently a member of Mount Calvary Baptist Church in West Palm Beach, Florida, where Bishop W. Oshea Granger serves as her Pastor. Evangeline is a member of the Mount Calvary Ministerial Staff, the Lead Servant over the "Living Single" Adult Singles' Ministry and faithfully serving within the Christian Education Department as a Sunday School, Bible Study, and School of Ministry Instructor.

God has tremendously blessed Evangeline with the gift to touch people and encourage the Kingdom of God by teaching through writing. Consequently, with a humble spirit and an ever so grateful heart, it is indeed a pleasure to announce that Evangeline became a published author in July 2013, with the release of her first book entitled <u>Intimate Moments.</u> Additionally, through God's guidance, in July 2020 Evangeline became the founder/president of the non-profit organization *Intimate Moments Ambassadors, Inc.* A Ministry that was founded under the principles of love. Evangeline has been tasked to teach the principles of love and how they relate to "Love & Relationships" under God's Design to the world.

Evangeline, affectionately known as Angie and "Pumpkin" to her family and friends, finds that her greatest joy and passion in life include serving God, especially when working and laboring in the midst of her specific God given assignment, cooking, singing, taking photographs, and spending quality time with family and friends.

Evangeline's favorite scripture is Galatians 6:9, "And
let us not grow weary while doing good, for in due season
we shall reap if we do not lose heart." (NKJV)

Ways to contact and connect with Evangelist Evangeline Rentz:
Email: angie0710@yahoo.com; Facebook:
intimate moments@angie765;
Address: Post Office Box 15683, West Palm Beach, FL 33416

Acknowledgements

Thank you, Lord, for another opportunity to share Your word and Your message. I am truly humbled to be chosen for Your use. To my family, I thank God for you, your continued love and consistent support mean more to me than I will ever be able to express in words. I am so thankful to God for the gift of my family. You guys are absolutely amazing.

To Linda Blackshear Smith: I am truly grateful for your presence in my life. What a **mighty force** and undeniable earthly example of God's Love that you are. Thank you for being a constant, steadfast, dependable, and unmovable friend, and mentor. You are the epitome of a true Sister "in Christ". Your love, support, encouragement, prayers, and counsel are appreciated more than I could ever explain. I love you dearly and I am so grateful to share this "island" with you.

To Ma Beamon and Ma Atkins: God truly favored my life when He blessed it with your presence. Although you did not give birth to me, you call me daughter and I am overwhelmingly thankful. My life was truly shattered on January 11, 2020 when my precious biological mother Annie Mae Rentz went home to be with the Lord. Yet, God had already strategically placed you in my life for reason and purpose. No, not to replace mama, but to continue to cover her child with the mothering wings of love, prayer, wisdom, encouragement, support, and counsel. I thank you for embracing me into your hearts and family. I can say with confidence that Mama was thankful for you. I know in my heart that she is proud that you are looking out for her child and that she was so very grateful that God designed and specifically chose you for my life.

To Bishop, W. Oshea Granger and Pastor Katrina Granger:

Thank you for your prayers, love, and support. I am truly grateful that you allow me the opportunity to serve in the local church and to freely operate in my gift and the ministry assignment that God has assigned to my life. I am eternally grateful.

To my extended family, friends, and church family: I am truly grateful for your love and continued support. I cannot begin to imagine what life would be without the help and encouragement of you guys … and you know exactly who you are. If I had ten thousand tongues, I still could not adequately thank God enough for your presence in my life. A special shout-out to some very special ladies; Evangelist Linda Blackshear Smith, Sister Evelyn Stevens, and Sister Charlene Waters for your selfless sacrifice in pre-reading this book, your invaluable input, editing recommendations, and your inspiring encouragement to complete this project. Oh, how grateful I am to have been blessed with your presence in my life.

Lastly, I am especially grateful and overwhelmingly thankful for the readers. I pray this book blesses your life and encourages you to actively prepare for your special wedding day!

Evangeline